LILLIAN T
JENNIFE

2011

fortune & feng shui

TiGER

Congratulations!

I want to thank and congratulate you for investing in yourself...and in the latest edition of Fortune and Feng Shui...your personalized horoscope book for 2011!

What will you be earning one year from today? How will you look and feel one year from today...and will you be happier?

In this little book Jennifer and I reveal many insights pertaining to your particular animal sign...what you can expect and how to protect and enhance all areas of your life for success in 2011.

And why stop here?

I'd like to also extend a personal invitation to you to join my Mandala...and receive my FREE online weekly newsletter...Lillian Too's Mandala Ezine.

You'll discover other powerful feng shui secrets from me that go hand-in-hand with the valuable information in this book. And it's absolutely FREE... delivered to your inbox weekly!

Lillian Too's Online Weekly Ezine... FREE!

You've taken the first step to success by purchasing this book. Now expand your horizons and learn more about authentic feng shui that really works...including more about the powerful 3rd dimension...your inner feng shui! Just go to www.lilliantoomandalaezine.com and register today!

It's EASY! It's FREE! It's FRESH and it's delivered to you WEEKLY

Don't miss out! It's easy to register at www.lilliantoomandalaezine.com and you'll also receive a special BONUS from me when you register today! I look forward to visiting with you online!

All the best!
Lillian

Fortune & Feng Shui 2011 TIGER
by Lillian Too and Jennifer Too
© 2011 Konsep Lagenda Sdn Bhd

Text © 2011 Lillian Too and Jennifer Too
Photographs and illustrations © WOFS.com Sdn Bhd

The moral right of the authors to be identified as authors of this book
has been asserted.

Published by KONSEP LAGENDA SDN BHD (223 855)
Kuala Lumpur 59100 Malaysia

For more Konsep books, go to www.lillian-too.com or www.wofs.com
To report errors, please send a note to errors@konsepbooks.com
For general feedback, email feedback@konsepbooks.com

ISBN 978-967-329-050-5
Published in Malaysia, August 2010

TIGER BORN CHART

BIRTH YEAR	WESTERN CALENDAR DATES	AGE	KUA NUMBER MALES	KUA NUMBER FEMALES
Fire Tiger	13 Feb 1926 to 1 Feb 1927	85	2 West Group	4 East Group
Earth Tiger	31 Jan 1938 to 18 Feb 1939	73	8 West Group	7 West Group
Metal Tiger	17 Feb 1950 to 5 Feb 1951	61	5 West Group	1 East Group
Water Tiger	5 Feb 1962 to 24 Jan 1963	49	2 West Group	4 East Group
Wood Tiger	23 Jan 1974 to 10 Feb 1975	37	8 West Group	7 West Group
Fire Tiger	9 Feb 1986 to 28 Jan 1987	25	5 West Group	1 East Group
Earth Tiger	28 Jan 1998 to 15 Feb 1999	13	2 West Group	4 East Group

CONTENTS

1. RABBIT YEAR 2011 - GENERAL OUTLOOK
Drastically Clashing Elements with Potential for Wealth

2. TIGER ENJOYS VICTORY ENERGY IN 2011

3. DISCOVERING YOUR LUNAR MANSION
The Influence of your Sky Animal

4. INTERACTING WITH OTHERS IN 2011
Your Confidence & Winning Attitude Inspires

5. MONTHLY ANALYSES OF YOUR LUCK
Good Timing Helps You Actualize
Big Auspicious Luck

6. IMPORTANT FENG SHUI FOR 2011

7. POWERFUL TALISMANS & AMULETS FOR 2011

RABBIT YEAR 2011
Clashing Elements
But Economically Better

The Year of the Golden Rabbit 2011 will be a noisy year filled with the sounds of clashing elements. Global energy continues to be discordant. But it is a year when most animal signs enjoy the potential to make genuinely good advances economically. There is money to be made. In fact, for those who are able to tap into their veins of good fortune, 2011 can turn out to be a bonanza year.

> 2011 is a year that favors animal signs located in the secondary compass directions and is less favorable to those occupying cardinal directions. So two thirds of the animal signs can look forward to improving their financial situation.

We examine three important indicators to determine the year's outlook when the diplomatic, soft-hearted Rabbit rules, taking center stage and bringing a new set of energies to the fortunes of the world. After the dramatic earthquakes, landslides and volcanic eruptions of the Tiger Year, can we welcome in a quieter, safer and more stable year? Alas, if the charts are any indication, it seems not; there are deep rumblings under the earth; natural disasters and discordant chi continues to pose a threat to our safety; these calamities threaten different parts of the world. Earth's environment needs time to settle but for most individuals, happily the outlook does not look that dire. There is more good luck than bad for most of the animal signs.

Outlook for the 12 Animals

In 2011, the Tiger benefits from the number 1 *Victory Star* which brings good feng shui winds of success and achievement. You will benefit from generating heaven luck energy by wearing the **Heaven Seal**. This is a year when depending on your own instincts will bring good fortune. For you, the 24 mountains constellation bring both good and bad, on your left is the *Five Yellow* while on your right is the *Big Auspicious*. So getting your timing right and thinking clearly is important. Make sure to always carry the **heaven seal amulet** to attract the positive rather than the negative. It also does not hurt to place the remedy to suppress the five yellow in the East corners of rooms you use frequently.

The **Rat** and the **Horse** (Tiger's ally) enjoy the promise of great good fortune, and whether or not they can actually cause this good luck potential to materialize will depend on their own inventiveness. But doing well in 2011 does not come without a share of the year's discordance. The Horse has a tendency to get sick, while the Rat's normally calm demeanor is put out of sorts by quarrelsome impulses brought by the hostility star.

Two other animal signs enjoying excellent potential are those born in the years of the **Dog** (Tiger's ally) and **Boar** (Tiger's secret friend), although for them, success luck can diminish if they are affected by discordant forces in their personal charts or simply have outdated feng shui in the home or they get hit by annual flying stars. The Boar needs to stay updated and be careful not to have good potential blocked by the year's afflictive energies. They should check to make sure that neither their main door nor their bedrooms are afflicted this year.

The cardinal East and West rulers, **Rabbit** and **Rooster** are afflicted by harmful energy and need to stay alert. These two must watch their backs, as both signs are affected. East and West are strongly afflicted directions. The **Rabbit** in 2011 is hit by the nasty *wu wang* or five yellow which is a powerful feng shui affliction. This is a negative star number that brings ill winds of misfortune and it must be strongly subdued. The **Rooster** meanwhile sits on the *Disaster Energy Star* in the West and must contend with the *Three Killings* affliction. These are bad winds which must also be subdued before Rooster can benefit from favorable feng shui brought by the number 9 star.

The **Snake** continues to have a good year in 2011 as it benefits from excellent feng shui winds. This is a year when continuous good fortune comes and brings big as well as small successes. The Snake enjoys excellent indications of good fortune brought by the 24 Mountain stars. Snake will definitely be on a roller coaster ride in 2011.

The **Ox** enjoys a wonderful year as it benefits from the double *Big Auspicious* stars that flank its astrological location. This together with its number 1 star ensures that good fortune manifests strongly. Meanwhile, inviting a deity figure into the home brings good luck as the Ox has the *Golden Deity Star* in its chart this year.

The **Dragon** has an uneventful year. It should sail through 2011 with small luck. Success is limited, but there is little to cause them grief. For the Dragon, heaven luck shines bright, so there could be unexpected windfalls. It is a good idea to enhance for special luck to manifest. For them, wearing and displaying good luck charms are sure to be beneficial.

The **Sheep** benefits from the year but only when there is an adequate supply of Earth element energy, so this sign needs strengthening with the **Earth Seal**. It also pays to display and wear raw and natural quartz crystal.

The **Monkey** has a harder time staying ahead of the competition, especially those working professionally pursuing a career. Those doing business need to be careful not to get conned. This sign could fall victim to external politicking. The Monkey must be alert to false friends and ambitious colleagues. It is beneficial to carry amulets that fight against the evil eye!

The Evil Eye Hanging

PAHT CHEE CHART 2011 - GOLDEN RABBIT

HOUR	DAY	MONTH	YEAR
HEAVENLY STEM	HEAVENLY STEM	HEAVENLY STEM	HEAVENLY STEM
壬	庚	庚	辛
YANG WATER	YANG METAL	YANG METAL	YIN METAL
EARTHLY BRANCH	EARTHLY BRANCH	EARTHLY BRANCH	EARTHLY BRANCH
丙午	甲寅	甲寅	乙卯
FIRE HORSE	WOOD TIGER	WOOD TIGER	WOOD RABBIT

HIDDEN HEAVENLY STEMS OF THE YEAR

YANG FIRE YANG EARTH	YANG FIRE YANG EARTH YANG WOOD	YANG FIRE YANG EARTH YANG WOOD	YIN WOOD

The year is desperately short of EARTH ie Resource

The Year's Four Pillars

The first indicator we look at to get an overall feel for the destiny outlook for the year is the year's Four Pillars chart. This offers a snapshot of the year and reveals the hidden forces that affect the fortunes of the year. To know what's in store, we analyse the eight elements that dominate the four pillars i.e. the heavenly stems and the earthly branches that rule the chi energies of the year.

The preceding Tiger Year was a year of unstable earth disasters characterized by rogue waves in the seas and plenty of big earthquakes that began at the start of the year and continued on unabated through the year... from Chile to Japan to Turkey to Indonesia to China and Taiwan. Last year, hidden Earth energies rumbled and brought tragedy and disaster to many parts of the globe.

In this coming year 2011 of the Golden Metallic Rabbit, its Four Pillars Chart looks rather foreboding. In fact, the chart is indicating not one pillar of directly clashing elements, but FOUR!

Yes, all four of the pillars have discordant crushing energies, with three pillars indicating Metal crushing Wood, instantly telling us that the Rabbit of 2011 is not going to be a docile one. The remaining pillar has Water destroying Fire.

So in 2011, all four pillars that make up the Eight Characters chart of the year are showing direct clashes. This is a nasty indication and it is a clear warning for everyone to be careful and circumspect.

Travel and risk-taking are best kept to a minimum, and it is a good idea to be prepared at all times. It is not a year to tempt fate. This is a general but potent piece of advice for the year. Better to stay home than to travel. Better to stay safe than to take risks.

Just glance quickly at the chart and instantly you will see that in the DAY, MONTH and YEAR pillars, Metal is destroying Wood! These are direct clashes and here we see both yin and yang pillars having the same clashing characteristics.

And then in the HOUR pillar, Water is destroying Fire! Each one of the four pillars indicates extremely negative outlooks for the year; so from year start to year end, and affecting all age groups, hostile energies dominate. This has to be a record of some kind; to have all four pillars showing a clash of elements with the heavenly stem elements destroying the earthly branches in every single pillar of the chart.

Disharmony is thus the prominent force of the coming year and despite the Rabbit, usually an icon of diplomacy, it appears that feng shui cosmic forces this year bring plenty of high octane anger and intolerance. In addition, the chart also show the presence of two Tigers, which suggests that the Tiger energies of 2010 have not entirely abated. We face a scenario not unlike that of the previous year, but maybe worse; clashing elements are always indicators of hard times, so the energy of the year looks discordant.

The chart shows Metal and Wood dominating, with Metal energy having the upper hand. The essence of the year is Metal, but it is neither weak nor strong Metal. Although we see three Metal, the Water and Fire of the Hour Pillar destroys and weakens the Metal. And because there is no Earth element present in the chart, Metal lacks the resources to stay strong.

There appears then to be a lack of resources during the year, and this is another bad sign. The absence of Earth also suggests an unbalanced chart, which is another indication of turmoil.

With this obvious imbalance, the prevailing attitude during the year is one of unrelenting intolerance. There are three Metals indicating the presence of competitive pressures, but the strength of the Metals cannot be sustained because of the lack of Earth. This indicates that competitive pressures cannot be sustained and it is best to not be pushed into a corner by competitors. Try thinking outside the box instead of combating the competition!

The Good News

When we look at the hidden elements of the chart, the news for 2011 is not all bad. Underlying all the competing energy lies the potential for the creation of much new wealth. There is hidden Earth bringing unexpected resources to fuel growth for the year, and there is also hidden Wood, indicating unexpected wealth. Likewise, there is also hidden Fire, so the year does not lack for managerial capability. The exercise of authority and leadership plays a big role in transforming the cosmic forces in 2011.

Results may not be evident in the year itself, but there is no denying the positive benefits of good leadership. As the Northwest patriarchal sector this year has the number 8, the cosmic forces are aligned to help the patriarchs i.e. the leaders of the planet. So in the trinity of heaven, earth and man, *tien ti ren*, it will be Mankind energy that prevails and delivers success and results.

Herein lies the good news for those who are commercially minded and business motivated. 2011 is a year when prosperity luck is present. There are many direct as well as indirect wealth-making opportunities emerging.

Although what is apparently missing are direct resources, as indicated by the element Earth which is missing from the main chart, there are thankfully three hidden Earth element. This more than makes up for their absence in the main chart. In effect, the chart can now be said to be balanced with the presence of all five elements, when the hidden elements are taken into account.

What *is* in very small supply however is the element of Water, which was completely missing last year.

In 2011, Water represents creativity, intelligence and common sense. Because it is in such short supply, everyone once again continues to benefit from the Water element. This is what will create Wood which stands for wealth this year. Water also exhausts Metal which is destroying the Wood element.

Thus the source of wealth creation in 2011 is Water; i.e. creativity - original and strategic thinking which will open the way to mining the year's prosperity. Much of this creativity will come from the younger generation.

This will be a year when those who have just joined the workforce, and those who have recently graduated out of school and College will be the source of new ideas. And because it is the year of the Rabbit, when the East sector comes into prominence, it is likely that those born as eldest sons of their families are the ones whose stars shine brightly. The year benefits the eldest sons of families.

Rabbit Years have always been years of appeasement, when conflicts arising in preceding Tiger Years get resolved. Unfortunately, 2011 continues to be a year of global political upheavals.

For the Tiger-born, the heavenly seal star protects against becoming a victim of the year's discordance.

But the Golden Rabbit Year is challenging and full of intrigues. Unlike the direct confrontations of the previous year, this is a year when unexpected betrayals and underhand tactics become prevalent. For the Tiger, you can easily cope with any kind of underhand attacks as you have the instincts to smell these out. Those feeling this darker side of the year's energy need to have a positive and non-defeatist attitude; only then can the coming twelve months from February 4th 2011 to February 4th 2012 benefit you. Then in spite of discordant element indications, you can create and accumulate new assets.

There is wealth luck in 2011. The Tiger can harness wealth luck, but only by making sure it taps into the luck of its heaven seal. What is needed is a keen eye for opportunities. Think outside the box to create new markets for your service and your products. The global business scenario is changing fast. New technology and applications of this fast-developing new technology is racing ahead at breakneck speed.

Globally, there is more than one prominent player in the technology game. Increasingly the world is feeling the presence of China. Note that Period 7 benefitted the West, but it is the Northeast that is ruling the energies of the current Period 8. This Period favors China. Both the year 2011 and the Period itself favors those who move fast; have prepared themselves to penetrate uncharted territory, just like water. We borrow the term blue oceans to suggest the clever opening up of new areas for creating wealth. And it does not matter whether you live in the West or in the Northeast, if you can work with the cosmic forces of the year and the period, you are sure to benefit.

Water is Vital

This is once again a year when the Water element brings prosperity, although not in the same way it did in the previous year. Those of you who installed water features last year and benefited from them will benefit again from it.

Note that in 2011, we are seeing three Metal destroying three Wood - i.e. clashing directly. The Metal of the year's heavenly stems continues to destroy the intrinsic Wood of the earthly branches. On the surface, this is not a good sign.

But Metal, when used with skill and under special circumstances, can transform Wood into something of greater value. So even as Metal destroys Wood, it can transform Wood into an object of value.

What is great for this year is that there is more than enough Wood around to make up for whatever gets destroyed. Note from the Pillars chart there are three hidden Wood element, so there is definitely wealth to be created and accumulated.

But clashing elements always suggest hostilities, so the wars of the world will not see any easing or closure. In 2011, fighting continues with little hope for reconciliation; competition in the commercial environment and between companies and countries will get worse. The energies of Heaven and Earth are clashing. So it is left to the energy of Mankind to make up for all the imbalances.

Mankind energy can be harnessed very effectively to overcome the discordant energies of heaven and earth this year. All the resources required are available, the only snag being they are hidden and so, not immediately obvious. But they are there!

Here we can use the third dimension of feng shui - the powerful inner chi dimension - to transform and enhance the space and time chi of 2011 at individual personalized levels. Irrespective of the discordance of Heaven and Earth, those of us who know how can still arrange our lives to benefit from the hidden forces of the year. We can focus on the mankind chi within all of us, concentrate on strengthening it, and in so doing, more effectively harness the spiritual energy of the empowered self to overcome obstacles and emerge triumphant.

There are methods and rituals we can use to subdue negative energies caused by the four sets of clashing elements. We can also apply element therapy to bring about a much improved balance in the elements in our immediate environments; and in addition, there are symbolic cures that are made into amulets and talismans that can subdue the negative "stars".

The Commanding Star

A very positive aspect of the year 2011 is the appearance of the *Commanding Star*, which is an outstandingly auspicious star. Its appearance in the 2011 chart is brought about by the presence of the Earthly Branch of Horse in the Hour pillar and the Earthly branch of Tiger in the Day pillar. This excellent indication arises out of the ally relationship that exists between Horse and Tiger. Here the Commanding Star suggests traits brought by these two fearless animal signs to the year. It brings good vibrations benefiting those who show courage and fortitude.

The Commanding Star suggests the presence of authority, power and influence luck for the year, benefiting those who find themselves in a leadership situation or those holding a position of authority. Indeed, the year will benefit those who know how to use their positions of influence and power; so managers and leaders who have a clear idea what their strategy or focus are will benefit from this star - despite the clashing elements of the year.

Leaders will find the energy of the year increases their charisma and their effectiveness. The exercise of authority will come easily. Those born in the years of the Tiger are especially blessed as it has the strength to absorb the power chi of the Northwest. In 2011 it enjoys the white star of 1 which has a natural affinity to the star of 8. Hence Tiger patriarchs can tap into the highly energized Chien trigram of the Northwest.

As such you, the Tiger person, have every reason to stand tall and succeed in 2011; With the help of the heaven seal and your own inner energy, you can make the effort to multiply your own resources and achieve your goals. Tiger is in a commanding position this year.

What can be worrying about the Commanding Star is that both the elements of the Hour pillar - Water and Fire - are not good for the intrinsic element of the year. Here we see Fire destroying Metal, and Water exhausting Metal. Superficially then, it appears that the Commanding Star can turn ugly, bringing obstacles instead of opportunities. For the Tiger however, there is nothing to fear. This is because the very essence and nature of the Commanding Star arises from the presence of both Tiger and Horse (its ally) in the paht chee chart of the year. The Tiger (with its ally) is thus in control of this powerful star. There is thus little danger of the Commanding star turning ugly for the Tiger.

In fact, there are two Tigers in the year's chart which adds strength to this great beast. This means that the Tiger person has enough chi energy to overcome whatever bad luck crosses its way.

Flying Stars of 2011

The feng shui chart of the year which lays out the location of the year's flying stars in 2011 is dominated by the energy of 7, a weak star; but being the reigning number, its effect cannot be overlooked. The number 7 is a Metal number that represents the negative side of relationships, symbolizing duplicity and treachery. The number adds fuel to the discordant vibes of the clashing elements of the Four Pillars.

So even though the Rabbit Year is usually a subdued one, 2011 has its full share of confrontation; global incidence of violence is likely to continue.

FLYING STAR CHART 2011 - GOLDEN RABBIT

SE	SOUTH	SW
SMALL AUSPICIOUS	BIG AUSPICIOUS	EARTH SEAL
6	2	4
SMALL AUSPICIOUS	BIG AUSPICIOUS	ROBBERY STAR
TAI SUI		
5	7	9
FIVE YELLOW		3 KILLINGS
HEAVEN SEAL	BIG AUSPICIOUS	YEARLY CONFLICT
1	3	8
GOLDEN DEITY	BIG AUSPICIOUS	YI DUO STAR
NE	NORTH	NW

EAST (left side) WEST (right side)

This is a year when intrigue and situational upheavals occur frequently; brought by a higher occurrence of betrayals and unbridled ambitions. It is a year when the center of buildings, houses and offices benefit from Water energy to subdue the strength of 7. Luckily, the number 7 is a weak star in the current Period of 8, so it is not difficult to subdue. Anything of a dark blue color is sufficient for keeping it under control. It is advisable to make the effort to suppress the number 7 in homes and offices. This brings protection for residents and prevents them from falling victim to external politicking and trouble-making people.

In 2011 it is a great idea to activate the power of Water in the home. Invest in a small water feature to create a small presence of moving water in the center grid of the home. Or place a **Rhino or Elephant** there. Together, these three remedies are excellent for suppressing the negative influence of 7.

The luck of the different sectors of any structure is influenced by the new energy brought by the year's feng shui chart, as this reveals the year's lucky and unlucky sectors for buildings, houses and apartments.

The chart for 2011 indicates different numbers in each of the nine grids in this three-by-three sector chart. This looks like the original Lo Su square which plays such a big role in time dimension feng shui except that each year, the numbers placed in each grid change according to the center number. With 7 in the center, the other numbers are then placed around the grid sectors. This is what changes the pattern of energy in homes and offices from year to year.

The numbers play a big part in determining the "luck outlook" of animal signs arising from the fact that each of the twelve signs occupies a designated compass location. Thus the Tiger person occupies the Northeast location and we can see from the chart that Tiger people enjoy the winning star of 1. This is a victory star! Your sign also enjoys a couple of excellent stars brought by the 24 mountains, one of which is the *Star of Big Auspicious.*

The stars of the 24 mountains are influential. There are 108 different fortune stars but only a handful fly into the 24 mountain directions in any year. These bring auspicious or harmful influences, but they vary in strength and type each year. For the Tiger this year, there is good and bad. We have noted the good big auspicious. What must be suppressed is the five yellow.

Houses and animal signs are affected in the same way by the 24 mountain stars. Some stars bring good luck, some bring misfortune. When your sign is negatively afflicted and your vitality gets weakened, you need to wear specific protective Taoist charms. These protect you from the affliction or they reduce its effects.

We have made different charms to match each animal sign's needs. What you, the Tiger needs is the five element pagoda with the tree of life mainly for placement in the East as well as Northeast sector of your home. But you should also get the heaven seal as this activates the star you are sitting on. There are also other talismans to attract good fortune. These are highlighted in Section 7 of the book. Remember to stay strong and fit through the year. Take care of the side five yellow causing you some aggravations ad then focus on making the best of the year.

Not many people know that it is essential to be mentally and physically strong to attract good fortune. After making sure that afflictions are suppressed you can attract good feng shui with powerful symbols of good fortune. But for these to be effective you need to stay healthy and confident. Your confidence must not get undermined by the side five yellow, so stay optimistic and maintain good health through the year.

This is what brings you the yang vigor needed to actualize good fortune. This helps to generate the third dimension to your luck - which is the empowerment of the self. It is this that makes the difference between succumbing to bad luck or transforming it into good luck. The process of transformation requires powerful self empowering energy. More on this later.

Staying Updated Each Month

Meanwhile, note that the monthly updates are just as important as the annual ones. Monthly luck forecasts are the highlight of this book because good timing plays an important part in attracting good fortune; and avoiding misfortunes. To enjoy good luck through the year, you must update your month to month feng shui. So you must keep track of how cosmic energies affect your luck each month

Every animal sign can be alerted to the high and low points of their year, and be warned against negative energy. As well as to spur you on during months when your chi energy is high. When to lie low and when to be go bravely forth are important to maximizing the opportunities of the year, so irrespective of whether the year is good or bad, you can avoid pitfalls and not miss out on chances that come your way.

Nothing beats being prepared against potential misfortune because this reduces their impact. Knowing the nature of misfortune - whether it is related to illness, or accident, betrayal or plain bad luck - helps you cope when the misfortune does occur. What is better is that when you wear protective remedies, mantra amulets or talismans, these are very effective in warding off misfortunes.

Thus an important aspect of reading these books is to take note of the spikes and dips in your monthly luck focusing on Career, Business, Family, Love and Study luck. The monthly readings analyze each month's Lo Shu numbers, element, trigram and paht chee luck pillars. These accurately identify your good and bad months; they generate valuable pointers on how to navigate safely and successfully through the year, effectively helping you get your timing right on important decisions and actions.

The recommendations in this book alert you to months when you are vulnerable to illness, accidents or dangers. We also highlight good luck months and this is when exciting new opportunities come to you. Knowing when will give you a competitive edge on timing. You will get better at coping with setbacks and overcoming obstacles that occur from month to month.

Improving Your Luck

Your luck can be substantially improved through the placement of symbolic enhancers or remedies in the spaces you occupy. This is a book on the personalized approach for you to attract good luck. You will see as you delve deeper into it, that there are many ways you can improve your personalized luck despite the year being afflicted for you.

What you need to place in your compass sector changes from year to year. You must be sure what exactly you need to place in your Northeast location in 2011, to suppress the side five yellow but more importantly to activate the luck of winning, and the chi of heaven. This year your luck is blessed by the year's flying stars (shown in the feng shui chart) as well as the four pillars and luck stars of the 24 mountains. How you react to the year's changing energies depends on the strength of your spirit essence and your life force.

This year, for all animal signs, both of these important indications stay the same as last year. There is no change to your life force and spiritual strength, so all Tiger sign people continue to experience the same energy as last year in these two areas. Only the success potential for everyone has changed. This section of the book has thus been shortened. In its place, we are introducing a new aspect that affects your fortunes.

The extra dimension we address this year is to introduce you to your SKY ANIMAL sign. In addition to your birth year animal sign, your destiny and attitudes are also influenced by your lunar mansion.

This is represented by one of the 28 sky animals that correspond to the 28 days in a typical month. This is your Day Sign and it interacts with your Year Sign to add new dimensions to your compatibility with others, and to your luck outlook each year.

Your Lunar Mansion

This is based on the four great constellations that are the foundation of feng shui - the constellations of the *Green Dragon, Crimson Phoenix, Black Tortoise* and *White Tiger*.

The **Green Dragon** rules the Eastern skies while the **Crimson Phoenix** rules the Southern skies. The **White Tiger** is the Lord of the Western Skies and the **Black Tortoise** oversees the Northern skies. Collectively, they rule over the 28 animals of the sky, each having dominance over 7 of these animals.

Depending on which of the 28 animals is your Day sign, you will be under the influence of (and thus protected by) the Dragon, the Tiger, the Phoenix or the Tortoise. In astrological terms, these are termed the constellations of the lunar mansion. Your Sky Animal brings additional insights to the kind of luck you enjoy in any given year depending on your profession or business. The year 2011 is ruled by the Eastern sign of the Rabbit; and with two Tigers in the Pillars chart, this is a year when the Green Dragon who rules the Eastern Skies is dominant. Those whose Day Sign comes under the mighty Dragon are more likely to benefit from the Dragon. Thus bringing the image of the Dragon into your home would be excellent.

The Dragon was very beneficial last year and continues to be the celestial creature that brings good fortune to the year 2011. And since the Water element continues to be in short supply, it is as beneficial to have water and Dragon together, especially in the East sector of your house where it enhances the Rabbit Year, working with the Tiger presence in the Pillars chart to create the Zodiac trinity combination of Spring.

The wearing of any kind of crystal or crystal embossed with Dragon or any kind of **Dragon jewellery** will be especially beneficial in 2011. Everyone will benefit from wearing big chunky natural quartz crystals in 2011 as this signifies the grounding Earth element that is missing from the Pillars chart. Earth is what provides the year's resources. It also strengthens the intrinsic element of the Dragon to balance the double Tiger hence transforming the year's Tiger energy to work powerfully in your favor.

It also combines with the Tiger to strengthen the Rabbit energy of the year. This will help to defuse the ferocity of the clashing elements at an individualized level.

Determining your lunar mansion Day Animal requires access to specific calculations retrieved from the Chinese Almanac.

In this book, these calculations have been simplified, and any one of you can quite easily work out your Day Animal sign from the chapter on your lunar mansion which also offers additional insights into your destiny outlook.

Updating Your Feng Shui

Buildings are affected by new energy patterns each year. Knowing how to work with these new energies is the key to unlocking good fortune in each new year.

It is important to place remedial updates that safeguard the feng shui of your home and office. This aspect of feng shui is its time dimension and because energy transforms at the start of the year, changing on the day of Spring popularly referred to as the lap chun, it is beneficial for all updates to be done before this date which falls on February 4th, 2011. This also corresponds to the start of the solar year of the Chinese Hsia calendar.

Remedial cures are always necessary to subdue the effects of negative stars and malicious influences of bad luck numbers in the flying star chart. The location and strength of these negative influences change from year to year so it is necessary to check them every year.

Three Dimensions in Feng Shui

Feng shui has three dimensions to its practice, a space, time and self-empowering dimension. These address heaven, earth and mankind chi that make up the trinity of luck that collectively account for how luck works for or against us. If you want to benefit from total feng shui, you should use the collective power of all three dimensions.

Space dimension is governed by environmental feng shui methods - collectively practiced under the broad umbrella of what everyone terms feng shui. Here, it comprises the art of living in harmony with natural landforms and the art of placing auspicious objects with great symbolic meaning and element properties around us. Environmental feng shui takes note of compass directions on a personalized basis and use other methods that focus on lucky and unlucky sectors. Broadly speaking, it takes care of the Earth aspect in the trinity of luck.

Then there is time dimension feng shui, which takes account of changing and transformational energies. This is founded on the premise that energy is never still; that it is constantly changing, and therefore we must see how energy transforms over overlapping cycles of time; annually, monthly, daily, hourly and even in larger time frames that last 20 years, 60 years and 180 years, which is the time it takes for a full nine period cycle of 20 years to complete. In this book, we focus on the all-important annual cycles of change, but we also look at the monthly cycles; and we write this book within the larger context of the Period of 8 cycle. Broadly speaking, time feng shui takes care of the *heavenly* cosmic forces that affect the trinity of luck.

Finally, there is the self or spiritual dimension, which broadly speaking depends on the energies generated by *Mankind*. This focuses on the chi energy individually and collectively created by people themselves. How we each individually, and together with others who live with us, empower the energy of self to either create good or bad energy in our living and work space.

In its highest form, the Self energy is believed to be the most powerful of all, and in the face even of extremely challenging **Heaven Luck** as is the case in 2011, the highly empowered self or highly focused person who has the ability to use the powerful forces of his/her mental concentration can indeed generate the all-powerful **Mankind** chi that can subdue afflictions brought by the intangible conflicting energy of the year's forces (**Heaven Luck**) as well as tangible bad energy caused by bad feng shui (**Earth Luck**).

The highly empowered self does not just happen; this too requires learning, practice and experience, and it involves developing a strongly focused and concentrated mind that can itself generate powerful chi. This is spiritual chi that take years to develop, but there are methods - both gross and subtle - that can be used to generate powerful mankind luck.

These methods are referred to as *inner feng shui.* Traditional feng shui masters of the old school are great adepts at invoking the Taoist spiritual deities through meditative contemplations, reciting powerful prayers and mantras and using purification rituals to remove obstacles.

Many turn to Buddhist deities who are believed to be very powerful in helping to awaken the inner forces within us. A great deal of feng shui history is thus tied up with Taoism and Buddhist practices in ancient China. However, this aspect of feng shui is usually kept secret by the Masters, many of whom are also expert at meditation techniques. It is meditation that enables them to access their highly empowered inner chi which brings their practice of feng shui to a much higher level of accomplishment.

We found that powerful ancient rituals for overcoming life obstacles such as those using incense and aromas and holy objects to enhance the spiritual energy of homes found their way to Tibet during the Tang dynasty where they were incorporated into their spiritual Buddhist practices, especially those that invoked the powerful earth Protectors of the Land of Snows. These rituals are now being revealed to the world by the high lamas of Tibetan Buddhism.

In 2011, it will be especially effective in practicing this method of feng shui, as it will alleviate many of the discordant energies of the coming year.

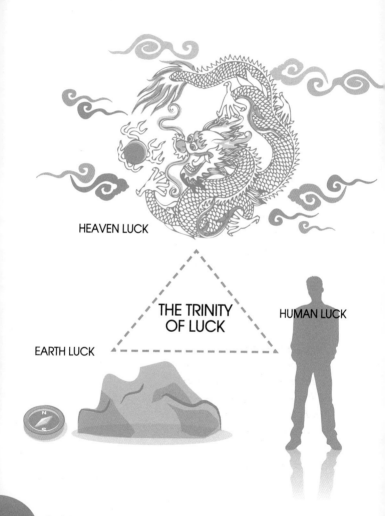

HEAVEN LUCK

THE TRINITY
OF LUCK

HUMAN LUCK

EARTH LUCK

Tiger enjoys Victory Energy in 2011

Part 2

STAYING ON TOP OF YOUR HOROSCOPE LUCK

- Metal Tiger – 61 years
- Water Tiger – 49 years
- Wood Tiger – 37 years
- Fire Tiger – 25 years
- Earth Tiger – 13 years

Outlook for the Tiger In 2011

The Tiger sign benefits from the victory white star number 1 in 2011; this normally sets the stage for some exciting triumphant moments as the number 1 star is one of three auspicious number stars in the annual flying star chart. For the Tiger, the potential looks good for achieving goals or for coming first, being the winner in competitive situations.

Success in getting what you want improves quite considerably this year, helped very likely from the great support you are getting from *Heaven Seal* luck in the constellation of the 24 mountain stars; this changes every year and in 2011, the Tiger is sitting on the *Star of Heaven Seal*. The Tiger receives the approval of heaven energy, and this attracts some kind of high level support.

It is possible that you unknowingly made a good impression on someone influential and this brings you unknown and unobserved mentor luck. Those of you who are feeling dissatisfied with life or feeling frustrated in your work environment should get a boost from the heaven seal. Activate this by getting just such a seal to stamp "*heaven*" in your diary, journal or notebook. This is sure to jumpstart something new and exciting for you.

The Tiger sign's luck in 2011 also benefits from the *Star of Big Auspicious* on its right; suggesting that at least one BIG thing coming to you this year. This could be brought by someone born in the year of the Ox. On balance however, it does seem that the year of the Rabbit will be very fruitful for the Tiger. There are some negatives you might want to take note of.

Watch that you do not get indirectly affected by the star of five yellow, which is not quite in your sphere but nevertheless can pose some danger. This appears on your left near to the Rabbit location; so do not hook up or get involved with someone from this sign this year. Also use the cure designed to suppress the negative influence of the five yellow for you to evade its aggravations causing effect.

The Tiger sign is characteristically courageous, a sign which suggests someone not afraid to take risks or move into uncharted new territory. The Tiger is a careful person not prone to impulsive behaviour and in a year of danger with natural calamities and plenty of conflict and strife, such as 2011 is, the Tiger would instinctively move carefully. Remember that the Tiger is an animal of the wild who stalks his prey with great patience and stealth.

In the paht chee cart of 2011, the presence of Tiger energy is very strong which suggests that all the attributes of this sign are quite pronounced. Everyone born under its sign and influence are certain to move very cautiously. What is comforting to take note of is that the Tiger is not lacking in inner spiritual essence despite a low life force indication it its horoscope element showing for the year. This is similar to the previous year except that then, the Tiger was affected by the illness star. So on balance you are much stronger this year and hence, in less danger than the previous year. It is likely that you will reap the fullest benefits of the lucky star number 1.

Not so lucky Tigers could get indirectly hit by the side five yellow which might bring illness or short term obstacles. This brings aggravating situations with setbacks to what you do, forcing you several steps backwards. Take care of this by placing the **five element pagoda** with the **tree of life** on the East side of your home. This remedy is excellent for subduing the five yellow.

The 49 year old **Water Tiger** benefits very much from its heavenly stem of water, as this brings some exceptional financial luck this year. Money comes quite effortlessly. This, added to the *Star of Big Auspicious* brought by the 24 mountains next to your sign should create big income luck for you. So for Water Tigers, the mercurial water brings enhancement to everything you do this year. You could actually experience some positive developments of nature that brings far reaching results. Of all the Tigers, yours will be the most high profile success.

The **Fire Tiger** also enjoys good financial luck combined with excellent health. At 25 years old, your wait for the big break could well be just at the edge of the horizon. If something amazing comes along, do make sure you stay focused and do not forget your due diligence.

Whether it be a matter of changing jobs, moving location, changing your lifestyle such as making a commitment or investing in a new business, it benefits to think things through and resist any impulsive urge to dive headlong in. Do remember always that big decisions can be transformative but how they eventually turn out is as much a function of luck as it is what you bring to the follow through to those decisions.

Money is not difficult to make, but it is beneficial to make its flow in your life stable and consistent. It will benefit you to be analytical. We are of course living through a time of massive change. It will be up to you to ensure you do not miss out on harvesting the goodies brought by these changes.

But money luck for the 61 year old **Metal Tiger** is low and for 37 year old **Wood Tiger** is dismal. It is likely that whatever auspicious luck comes to you will not necessarily be in the form of added net worth. More likely for you in 2011 we are looking at some meaningful personal triumph and victory.

The overall outlook for all Tigers this year is very exciting. Obstacles that manifest will be minor, actually bringing inconvenience more than any serious loss. You will have few problems negotiating through the day-to-day grind of living but be prepared for the unexpected. Big things can come wrapped in unattractive packaging and vice versa. Get the heaven seal and stamp it brightly on all your correspondence to create your own awareness and be alert to new people and opportunities.

The Tiger Personality in 2011

The sign of the Tiger famously signify the finer qualities of mankind. There are magnificent metaphors linked to the Tiger's sense of honour and its valiant ferocity - these are almost always seen in a favourable light. The Tiger is brave, protective of loved ones and in a competitive situation almost always emerges victorious. To the Tiger winning is often a life and death kind of obsession and this is not surprising of course. In the wild, the hunt for food is a very serious matter!

But almost all Tigers have their Achilles heel, some sort of weakness which make them vulnerable -- this sort of describes Tiger's energy in 2011, very strong and powerful but also vulnerable. Its weakness probably lie in its usually hidden expressions of compassion.

The Tiger personality is kind and often generous with friends and family, but rarely likes being seen this way. The Tiger is also always willing to take the blame; reflecting its broad and hefty shoulders. Its protective nature, especially to family and loved ones is instinctive even though it can quite coolly be hurting them in other ways and not realizing this.

As a result, those close to the Tiger person but with whom they have yet a level of intimacy tend to view them as cold and insensitive. Whenever something goes wrong however, the Tiger rarely looks for someone on whom to pin the blame. Instead, the Tiger almost always looks for solutions, and the faster the better. In this respect, this is a practical action-oriented sign who rarely means anyone any harm despite appearances to the contrary.

Not many people will see past the Tiger's strong survival instincts, nor get close enough to enjoy the Tiger's soft side. To see beyond the strength of your Tiger presence, others need to break through your competitive veneer. Scratch the surface and you will find someone clearly vulnerable. This was the case last year and continues to be the same this year, except that where in the previous year Tiger was weak and prone to sickness, this year Tiger becomes considerably stronger, rebounding with improved vitality and optimism.

As the year progresses, the Tiger's confidence recovers, so the aura around you will send out some clear and positive signals. There is an air of optimism which gets increasingly pronounced and whatever small misfortunes might recur, the Tiger will make good strides forward this year.

When doubts set in, just move with the flow and let the *Golden Deity* star and the signs of *Big Auspicious* take you where you will. This is a year to move in sync with the energy of heaven. Let this take you to new levels of awakening.

Outlook For Lady Tiger In 2011

BIRTH YEAR	TYPE OF TIGER LADY	LO SHU AT BIRTH	AGE	LUCK OUTLOOK IN 2011
1950	METAL TIGER LADY	5	61	Believing in herself brings victory
1962	WATER TIGER LADY	2	49	Excellent financial gains this year
1974	WOOD TIGER LADY	8	37	Benefiting from the water element
1986	FIRE TIGER LADY	5	25	Good prosperity and health
1998	EARTH TIGER LADY	2	13	Learning the ropes and winning

The Lady Tiger greatly recovers composure and strength and this translates into a more positive view of those around her. She develops a sense of greater security and her world view sees a positive change. With last year's illness star out of the way, she wanders further afield from her lair so the adventurous urge that has always lain latent within her emerges.

The Lady Tiger becomes more daring and adventurous; and this especially reflects the attitudes and personality of the Fire and Water Tiger females, the young 25 year old tentatively embarking on a career and the veteran 49 year old Tiger lady who is in her prime and knows it too. These are two Tiger ladies whose attainments of the previous year in financial undertakings make them extremely confident people 2011. Luckily for them both, there is big money luck and some excellent good health to boot. The Water Tiger lady will definitely emerge as someone to watch.

She may not have much in terms of direct and glamorous kind of success but behind the scenes this is lady pulling many strings. The Tiger woman's influence is pervasive in 2011 and any Tiger born woman who finds herself being put into the spotlight will see her views and opinions on many issues resonating with others. her influence will in fact be quite extensive indeed.

As for the other Tiger women, success and money might not be as impressive in 2011. To start with they will lack the vitality and the stature of the Fire and Water Tiger women. There could be a shortage of vitality which prevents their innate dominant nature to arise. For the 37 year old Wood Tiger, what you badly need is the element of water if money luck is what you want. In this year's horoscope, the element signifying wealth luck is Metal, which destroys the Tiger's Wood. Introduce water into your surroundings however, and it instantly subdues the metal while producing the wood. Create a water feature as soon as you can as water is as beneficial this year as it was last year. For 61 year old Earth Tiger on the other hand, wealth luck comes with enhanced Fire energy. make certain that your space is always well lit. If this does not improve your net worth during the year, it will at least ensure no loss.

Irrespective of how the year pans out however the Tiger female will rise to any challenge sent her way. The competitive spirit will rise as soon as she finds herself in any situation that contains elements of competition. The Tiger lady is at her best when she is all worked up. In 2011 she will not disappoint herself.

Outlook For Gentleman Tiger In 2011

BIRTH YEAR	TYPE OF TIGER MAN	LO SHU AT BIRTH	AGE	LUCK OUTLOOK IN 2011
1950	METAL TIGER MAN	5	61	Forging ahead despite setbacks
1962	WATER TIGER MAN	2	49	Financially an excellent year
1974	WOOD TIGER MAN	8	37	Benefiting financially from water
1986	FIRE TIGER MAN	5	25	Excellent money & health luck
1998	EARTH TIGER MAN	2	13	Emerging victorious brings a high

The Tiger gentleman will shrug off whatever feelings of doubts that may have caused them to feel nervous last year and find themselves revived by the strong gusts of some excellent feng shui winds this year. In 2011, sickness vibes which brought a lowering of resistance last year have faded. These have given way to the powerful star of victory which is both auspicious and extremely benevolent. The number 1 star is also a super confidence booster for this magnificent sign. Nothing makes a Tiger gentleman more manly, macho and strong as when they sense good times coming back. When the air is still and yin energy dominates the Tiger will instinctively hide, waiting for things to change before emerging into the sunlight.

In 2011, despite personal chi being at unimpressive levels in most of their luck categories, nevertheless, the feng shui chart and 24 mountain constellation more than makes up for this. As a result, the Tiger male transforms into a winner.

For the Earth, Metal and Wood Tiger guy s still lack the Fire and Water elements needed to bring better personal and direct luck. as a result direct success might still be hard to come by. Luckily for them not only is there the promising victory star but there is also the promise of something big coming your way. This is the big auspicious star coming from the Ox direction.

Thus in 2011 these Tigers need to keep their heads down. They should instead now follow their natural instincts and shake off any thoughts of failure. Good results are not that difficult to come by so if they allow their natural fighting instincts a longer rein, good results can come from them. The Tiger's inner strength works overtime, and excellent results are certain if these Tigers build a waterfall feature in their garden.
The Tiger males born with Fire and Water in their year of birth however the year brings exceptional wealth and health luck. For the 25 year old **Fire Tiger**, there is excellent health luck and positive money luck, so this is a very exciting year for you.

For the 49 year old **Water Tiger**, it will be even better, as the year 2011 continues to bring you excellent financial luck. Money flows to you effortlessly and health luck is also good. Last year's goodies simply will not stop and it is likely that everything will get even better yet.

Personal Horoscope Luck in 2011

The Tiger's Life Force luck is showing a single cross, X. This is a mild indication of there being some small danger in 2011. Usually this category of luck reveals if there are hidden dangers or threats to your life that might result in premature death or cause some suffering over a period of time.

When the year shows a higher incidence of natural disasters such as last year earthquakes and volcanic activity around the world, it is advisable to take this warning as timely. Natural calamities can bring havoc suddenly and unexpectedly and this year's paht chee chart indicates that this year, the world continues to be under a cloud of conflicting energy patterns.

As such, the single X in Tiger's horoscope reading should prompt you to put yourself under the protection of sacred talismans that contain powerful holy syllables and mantras. This is one of the easier and accessible ways of warding off dangers to your person. Wearing or carrying them should safeguard you.

Meanwhile, if you also do something good for charity, then whatever danger may be coming to your physical person will be efficiently averted. Threats to the Life Force are generally regarded as karmic ripening of some non-virtuous behaviour or transgression on your part in this or some past life so they can be assuaged by kind acts in this lifetime. So should any opportunity to help someone arise this year, grab the chance to do so.

The good news is that the Tiger's Spirit Essence is one circle O, which is a positive showing. This category of luck is in many ways more important and vital than other categories. It reveals insights into your inner resilience and spiritual strength in any year and when this inner essence is strong you are resistant to fears or any kind of nervousness. It also means a lower susceptibility to spiritual afflictions, and a stronger and more effective ability to overcome negative showings in other categories of luck. Circles suggest inner calm and one O indicates you are blessed. Your confidence level will be positive and it can pull out of any bad luck situation.

In terms of Health/Finance/Success Luck, this differs for each of the Tiger persons categorised according to age and the element of their heavenly stem. The luck ratings of everyone born in a Tiger year are presented in the tables below. These give a snapshot of your personal horoscope luck for 2011.

Earth Tiger - 73 & 13 Years Old

TYPE OF LUCK	ELEMENT AT BIRTH AFFECTING THIS LUCK	ELEMENT IN 2011 AFFECTING THIS LUCK	LUCK RATING
LIFE FORCE	Wood	Wood	X
HEALTH LUCK	Earth	Wood	XX
FINANCE LUCK	Earth	Metal	OX
SUCCESS LUCK	Metal	Fire	XX
SPIRIT ESSENCE	Water	Water	O

HEALTH LUCK - showing XX indicates disturbing health ailments.

FINANCE LUCK - showing OX means there is no discernible improvement in your economic status.

SUCCESS LUCK - showing XX decline over last year. Balanced by good showing of success in the feng shui chart.Luck in 2011

Metal Tiger – 61 Years Old

TYPE OF LUCK	ELEMENT AT BIRTH AFFECTING THIS LUCK	ELEMENT IN 2011 AFFECTING THIS LUCK	LUCK RATING
LIFE FORCE	Wood	Wood	X
HEALTH LUCK	Wood	Wood	X
FINANCE LUCK	Metal	Metal	X
SUCCESS LUCK	Metal	Fire	XX
SPIRIT ESSENCE	Water	Water	0

HEALTH LUCK - showing X indicates minor health ailments with the occasional bout of flu or muscular ache.

FINANCE LUCK - showing X means you could sustain a minor loss this year.

SUCCESS LUCK - showing XX decline over last year. Balanced by good showing of success in the feng shui chart.

Water Tiger – 49 Years Old

TYPE OF LUCK	ELEMENT AT BIRTH AFFECTING THIS LUCK	ELEMENT IN 2011 AFFECTING THIS LUCK	LUCK RATING
LIFE FORCE	Wood	Wood	X
HEALTH LUCK	Metal	Wood	OO
FINANCE LUCK	Water	Metal	OOO
SUCCESS LUCK	Metal	Fire	XX
SPIRIT ESSENCE	Water	Water	O

HEALTH LUCK - showing OO means you are in good health with no problems this year.

FINANCE LUCK - showing OOO means you enjoy a super year in terms of financial improvements.

SUCCESS LUCK - showing XX decline over last year. Balanced by good showing of success in the feng shui chart.

Wood Tiger – 37 Years Old

TYPE OF LUCK	ELEMENT AT BIRTH AFFECTING THIS LUCK	ELEMENT IN 2011 AFFECTING THIS LUCK	LUCK RATING
LIFE FORCE	Wood	Wood	X
HEALTH LUCK	Water	Wood	OX
FINANCE LUCK	Wood	Metal	XX
SUCCESS LUCK	Metal	Fire	XX
SPIRIT ESSENCE	Water	Water	0

HEALTH LUCK - showing OX suggests average health luck.

FINANCE LUCK - showing XX means your financial net worth could decline this year.

SUCCESS LUCK - showing XX decline over last year. Balanced by good showing of success in the feng shui chart.

Fire Tiger – 25 Years Old

TYPE OF LUCK	ELEMENT AT BIRTH AFFECTING THIS LUCK	ELEMENT IN 2011 AFFECTING THIS LUCK	LUCK RATING
LIFE FORCE	Wood	Wood	X
HEALTH LUCK	Fire	Wood	OOO
FINANCE LUCK	Fire	Metal	OO
SUCCESS LUCK	Metal	Fire	XX
SPIRIT ESSENCE	Water	Water	O

HEALTH LUCK - showing OOO suggests excellent health.

FINANCE LUCK - showing OO indicating good financial luck with increase in net worth possible.

SUCCESS LUCK - showing XX decline over last year. Balanced by good showing of success in the feng shui chart.

Discovering Your Lunar Mansion

Part 3

How Your Sky Animal Affects Your Luck

YOUR LUNAR MANSION is named one of 28 Sky animals that pinpoint the Day of the week that is favorable for you and more importantly it reveals what sky constellation you belong to thereby opening up a mine of information as to the kind of people you work best with; the area of work that offers the best potential for success; and the nature of the assistance your Sky animal brings you in any given year. Your lunar mansion is an integral part of you, so it deepens your understanding of what makes you tick; how it modifies the attitude tendencies and outlook for your Zodiac sign

There are **four Sky Constellations** under each of which are seven Sky Animals, three of them primary and four, secondary. Those of you born in a Tiger year will work well with Sky Animals belonging to the Eastern Skies and as a team or partnership, you attract good business luck. At the same time, your own Sky Animal will likewise determine which of other Sky Animals work well with you. Basically, these are colleagues belonging to the same constellation as you. Each constellation refers to one of four sections of the Skies, and these are associated with the four celestial guardians, the Green Dragon, who guards the Eastern skies, the Crimson Phoenix, who protects the Southern Skies, the Black Tortoise, lord of the Northern Skies, and the White Tiger, who rules the Western Skies.

The Celestials and the Sky Animals mirror the celestial guardians of feng shui and the Zodiac animal signs that make up the earthly branches of Astrology. This mirror effect strengthens specific types of good fortune. Sky Animals rarely bring obstacles as their effect is generally positive. They signify the influence of heaven.

Lucky Day

Everyone is born on a DAY that corresponds to one of these Sky Animals. In astrological terms, this is the lucky DAY for you. It is described as your corresponding lunar mansion and it reveals the influence of star constellations on your professional and business life from year to year. One's lunar mansion is analyzed in conjunction with one's personal Four Pillars chart and the Four Pillars chart of the year. Such a detailed analysis is not within the scope of this book, but it is useful to know the trends brought by the influence of your lunar mansion (or Sky Animal) in terms of your relationships and your luck in 2011.

Compatibility

For instance, everyone belonging to the same constellation and coming under the same Celestial Guardian has an affinity with each other, and in times of trouble, one can depend on the other, sometimes even in spite of them being opposing signs based on year of birth.

Sky Animals also have natural affinity to their corresponding Zodiac animal signs e.g. a Sky Tiger has affinity with someone born in the year of the Tiger and vice versa and the Sky Tiger also has affinity with someone born in the year of the Horse or Dog (Tiger's allies). This applies to all 12 animal Zodiac signs as each sign has a Sky counterpart!

Meanwhile, you can also be a secret friend of a Sky Animal. Thus the Sky Boar is the secret friend of the Tiger. This creates very powerful work luck as your heaven and earth chi blend well. This is a heaven and earth relationship. In itself, this is an indication of auspicious chi, so it is good for the Tiger to go into partnership with someone who is a Sky Boar.

Determining the Dominant Celestial Guardian

The coming year 2011 is a Rabbit Year with two Tigers and a Horse in its Pillars chart. This suggests that the Green Dragon who rules the Eastern Skies is dominant. This arises from it being a Rabbit Year and the Rabbit is one of the Sky signs belonging to the Dragon constellation.

The Dragon rules the Skies of the East and included in this constellation is also the Sky Tiger. The Zodiac Tiger whose location is part of the East also makes appearances in the year's paht chee.

The strength and influence of the Dragon's constellation is thus very powerful in 2011. It is definitely beneficial to invite the image of the Dragon into the home in 2011.

Note especially that in 2011, the lunar year begins on the **3rd of February** which corresponds to the day before the **lap chun**, the day of Spring. This is an auspicious indication. This could bring miracles to the year and help in transforming conflict energy into something productive.

With the Dragon as the ruling celestial guardian, growth energy during the year will be strong. The Sky Dragon is the key to subduing all discordant energies brought by the clashing elements on earth. Lining up all seven animals of the Dragon's constellation is believed to bring greater strength for getting projects started and attracting the good fortune of the Sky Dragon constellation. This applies to the Rabbit, its seasonal ally, the Dragon as well as to those born in the sign of the Tiger.

Even just placing the three main Sky signs of this constellation - the Dragon, Tiger and Rabbit -would be extremely auspicious and it benefits to place them in the East part of your garden or along an East wall of your living room. Sky signs look exactly like their Zodiac counterparts.

Green Dragon Constellation

The seven Sky animals that belong to the Dragon's constellation of the Eastern skies are the Sky Dragon, Sky Rabbit and Sky Tiger as well as the Sky Salamander, Sky Beaver, Sky Fox and Sky Leopard.

1. The Sky Salamander

This sky creature epitomizes the phenomenon of growth energy, associated mainly with agriculture and plantations. Any kind of profession associated with plants, gardens or plantations would be beneficial. This creature is a cousin of the Dragon but is also able to complement Tiger people. With this sign, you have strong creative instincts. You have good fortune in 2011 and heaven luck is good. Your lucky day is Thursday.

2. The Sky Dragon

This powerful creature is said to be a magician, able to create wondrous things out of nothing more than dreams. Success comes early in life and you could peak earlier than you wish. The Tiger born with this sign finds that pursuing their own ideas and believing in themselves is excellent strategy. You can take some risks this year and there could be good things coming your way in 2011. Stay relaxed! Your lucky day is Friday.

3. The Sky Beaver

This is a creature that signifies stability and good foundation. If this is your sign, you should seek out mentors, people senior to you who could bring you "*follow my leader luck*". A Tiger born with this Sky Animal sign usually benefits enormously because the Sky Beaver enhances your networking luck which will open pathways to many lucrative opportunities. Your lucky day is Saturday.

4. The Sky Rabbit

This is the most accommodating creature of this Constellation, usually associated with bringing family members together and establishing the bliss of domestic comforts. A Tiger born with this sign will put family above work in 2011. Your lucky day is Sunday.

5. The Sky Fox

This crafty, alert and quick witted creature works well with the character of the stealthy Tiger personality. Described as the heart and soul of the Dragon constellation, this creature can steer you to a high position and great success. An asset to any of the twelve signs of the Zodiac. Your lucky day is Monday.

6. The Sky Tiger

This is the creature is said to be born with a jade pendant on its forehead; so power and authority comes naturally to anyone who is a Sky Tiger. Success can be assured in the political arena and they also receive unexpected windfalls of luck all through their life, attracting help and support from family and friends. This lunar mansion identifies instantly with the Tiger-born, bringing you some auspicious luck in 2011. Your lucky day is Tuesday.

7. The Sky Leopard

This is the creature that benefits from being close to the Dragon; the wind beneath the sails, the faithful second in command. Sky leopards are almost always surrounded by many of the good things in life whether or not these belong to them. Nevertheless they are able to enjoy life's luxuries. The Tiger born as a Sky Leopard can achieve great success if they are discreet, loyal and keep their own counsel. Your lucky day is Wednesday.

Black Tortoise Constellation

For the Tiger-born, if your Sky Animal comes under the Tortoise constellation, you personify the good life with little effort. This creates energies that make it easy for you to take the fullest advantage of your good fortune indications in 2011. It becomes a double bonus this year.

The animals of the Tortoise Constellation are the Sky Ox (NE1), the Sky Rat (North), and the Sky Boar (NW3). There are also the Sky Unicorn, the Sky Bat, the Sky Swallow and the Sky Porcupine.

8. The Sky Unicorn

This creature combines the speed of the Horse with the courage of the Dragon. For the Tiger, if this is your Sky Animal, it indicates two extreme sides of you, for the Unicorn is at once your best friend and your own worst enemy. Tiger-born people whose Sky counterpart is the Unicorn could have an exaggerated sense of do-goodness about them. You have to look beyond small grievances and take the big picture approach to attaining all your dreams. Make sure you do not lose out on the main chance. Your lucky day is Thursday.

9. The Sky Ox

This creature is associated with the legend of the weaving maiden and the Ox boy forced to live apart and able to meet only once a year. Tiger-born people whose Sky Animal is the Ox can borrow Ox's extremely favorable luck in 2011, especially in real estate investments. The single Tiger could also find true love this year, but there might be small obstacles. Your lucky day is Friday.

10. The Sky Bat

This is a secondary sign of the Tortoise constellation but it is a symbol that signifies extreme good fortune. Benefits keep coming to you, especially if you are in the construction or engineering profession. Tiger-born with this Sky sign enjoy a life of comfort, living in a mansion through adult life. The Bat is greatly blessed if living in a temple or turns spiritual. There is good fortune awaiting you in 2011. Your lucky day is Saturday.

11. The Sky Rat

This sign signifies winter where yin energy rules. The Tiger whose Sky sign is the Sky Rat enjoys very auspicious luck brought by 2011. A very auspicious year awaits you. You will be on the receiving end of some good fortune. Your lucky day is Sunday.

12. The Sky Swallow

This is the sign often associated with foolhardiness and danger, as the swallow flies too fast and too high. This is the risk-taker of the Tortoise constellation and Tiger-born people having this Sky sign could be a little too impulsive, and as a result could rush into making ill-advised decisions. If this is your sign, it would be advantageous to reflect carefully before committing to anything new. Your lucky day is Monday.

13. The Sky Boar

This is a sign associated with the good life, which gets better as you get older. Tiger-born having this Sky sign are sure to be living in a mansion and feel very connected within themselves arising from the strong bonds between Boar and Tiger. You will enjoy good fortune in 2011 and the older you are, the better the luck coming your way. Good year to move into a bigger house. Your lucky day is Tuesday.

14. The Sky Porcupine

This is the policeman of this constellation, always conscious of security, alert to people with dishonest intentions.

Tiger-born people having this sign are artistic and hardworking, and very committed to what they do. This is a year when you can excel. Do not lose confidence in yourself in 2011, otherwise you might not have the courage to accept what comes your way. Your lucky day is Wednesday.

White Tiger Constellation

The White Tiger constellation tends to be vulnerable in 2011, hence those born into this grouping are advised to take things easy and lie low. The Mountain Stars affecting the Western skies are potentially disastrous, bringing misfortune. Taking risks could be dangerous and the year itself is already showing several warning signs, so it is best not to be too adventurous or foolhardy. Tiger-born people whose Sky Animal falls under this constellation are naturally alert to warning signs; they are the powerful hunters and protectors of the heavens and the earth and they know when to take the conciliatory approach and when to get their guard up. They know discretion is always the better part of valour. This is not a good year for these Sky Animals to be too aggressive or too adventurous. But being a Tiger-born, your year influence does give you added protection this year.

The Tiger's constellation has the Sky Dog (NW1), the Sky Rooster (West) and the Sky Monkey (SW3). On a compass you can see this reflects the Western skies sector. These are creatures of Autumn, when others are preparing to hibernate. In 2011, when the year is dangerous for this grouping of Sky Animals, it is a good time to stay less active.

The secondary Sky Animals of the Tiger Constellation - the Sky Wolf, Sky Pheasant, Sky Raven and Sky Ape, protect and support the main creatures with all seven coming under the care of the White Tiger. In astrological terms, the signs in the grouping of the Western Sky creatures are the most commercially-minded of all the Sky Animals. In 2011, protection is the keyword for those belonging to this constellation.

15. Sky Wolf

This is an insecure creature with a tendency towards negativity, expecting the worse to happen. The Sky Wolf requires plenty of reassurance and it is this lack of confidence that is its worst drawback. A Tiger who is a Sky Wolf must exert greater efforts to be upbeat especially in 2011. Confidence is the key to succeeding. Your lucky day is Thursday.

16. Sky Dog

This is an excellent sky sign as it indicates a life of success. The Sky Dog always has a pile of treasures at its feet; commercial and business success comes easily and effortlessly and theirs is a life filled with celebration and merry making. The Tiger who is also a Sky Dog can find success in 2011 benefiting from the stars of Big Auspicious. But you have conflicting emotions and you need to be careful this year. Your lucky day is Friday.

17. The Sky Pheasant

This is another extremely good Sky sign as the Pheasant indicates someone successful at creating and keeping their wealth. This is a Sky sign that is particularly suited to a career involving finance such as banking. This sign will also never be short of money as the Sky Pheasant attracts wealth continuously. The Tiger-born with this sign is sure to be rich but do be alert to anyone trying to con you of your money! Your lucky day is Saturday.

18. The Sky Rooster

This creature reflects its Zodiac counterpart, being naturally vigilant and watchful. The Sky Rooster is described as the eyes and ears of the skies, ever alert to those who would disturb the natural order. You are an excellent one to have around in 2011, which is a year when your instincts are at their most alert. Tiger-born with this Sky sign benefit from the special relationship between it and the Rooster; you will be going through risky but potentially prosperous times. Your lucky day is Sunday.

19. The Sky Raven

This is the creature of the Sky that signifies extremely rich rewards from efforts expended. The Sky Raven is associated with success of the most outstanding kind. As long as you are determined enough, you will get what you work for. Tiger born with this sign need to work hard to enjoy a fruitful year in 2011. Your lucky day is Monday.

20. The Sky Monkey

This is a natural born leader who assumes leadership responsibilities without hesitation, naturally extending protective arms outwards. They are thus charismatic and attractive. A Tiger born under the sign of the Sky Monkey will be a role model of some kind. Others are inspired by you. Your lucky day is Tuesday.

21. Sky Ape
This is the creature who signifies the important law of karma, ripening for them faster than for others. Thus Sky Ape succeed when they work and find life difficult when they slack off. Good deeds bring instant good rewards and likewise also vile deeds. A Tiger with this Sky sign will have good instincts in 2011. Your lucky day is Wednesday.

Crimson Phoenix Constellation
The Crimson Phoenix rules the Southern skies and its Sky Animals are the Sky Horse (South), Sky Sheep (SW1), and Sky Snake (SE3). As with the creatures of the other constellations, any family or business entity represented by this group of Sky Animals under the Phoenix benefit each other immensely. Collectively they attract exciting opportunities; their best time comes during the summer months and working on weekends benefits them. The Sky Animals or lunar mansions of the Southern skies are the:

22. Sky Anteater:

This is a creature that has the potential to exert great influence, but whether or not this can materialize depends on other factors. The Sky Anteater can be a catalyst, but it cannot initiate or spearhead a project or be a leader. But as someone supporting someone else, there is no better person. Tigers born with this Sky sign work well behind the scenes. Your lucky day is Thursday.

23. Sky Sheep

This Sky sign indicates someone who will eventually become deeply spiritual or psychic. When developed to its fullest potential, such a person becomes incredibly charismatic - easily becoming an iconic source of inspiration to others. A Tiger born with this Sky sign has the potential to achieve brilliance as industry leaders or politicians. Your lucky day is Friday.

24. Sky Roebuck

This is a creature of healing, someone who has the gift to mend broken hearts and emotionally distraught people. Those with this Sky sign have calm dispositions, so a Tiger born under this Sky sign will be an excellent calming influence on anyone. This sign usually does extremely well as counselors. Your lucky day is Saturday.

25. Sky Horse

This is a lovely Sky sign loved by many people. Also referred to as the mediator of the skies, the Sky Horse takes everyone for a joyride, helping others forget their grievances with great effectiveness. A Tiger born with this sign is adventurous and rebellious, feeling completely at home taking risks and venturing into the unknown. Your lucky day is Sunday.

26. Sky Deer

This is a generous creature whose spirit of giving endears it to many others. The Sky Deer is often associated with those who make it to a high position and then using their influence and success to benefit many others. A Tiger-born who has this Sky sign is sure to have this dimension of generosity in their personality. Your lucky day is Monday.

27. Sky Snake

This creature represents imperial authority. The Sky Snake travels on the wings of the Phoenix, always ready to receive applause and the adoration of others. Sky Snakes enjoy the destiny of amazing personal advancement especially in the political arena. A Tiger who is also a Sky Snake should watch for a good business opportunity to pursue in 2011. Your lucky day is Tuesday.

28. Sky Worm

Humble as this creature may sound, the Sky Worm aims high and when it succeeds it does so with panache and great style. This is the great surprise of the constellation of lunar mansions because those born under this sign have great perseverance and amazing courage to take risks; success for them comes with a vengeance! The Tiger with this sign should do well in 2011. Your lucky day is Wednesday.

Determining Your Sky Animal Sign

Example: If your day of birth is
25th October 1974

1. Get the corresponding number for your
   month and **year** from **Table 1**. Thus the
   number for October is **20**, and the number
   for the year 1974 is **13**.

2. Next, add the numbers of the month and
   the year to the day in October which is **25**.
   Thus **20 + 13 + 25 = 58**.

3. Next determine if your year of birth 1975 is
   a leap year; if it is, and you were born after
   March 1st, add 1. Here 1974 is not a leap
   year, and you were born after March 1st, so
   here you do not add 1 to **58**.

4. As **58** is more than **56**, you need to subtract
   56 from 68. Thus **58 - 56 = 2**. So note that
   for you, the Sky Animal is number **2**.

To explain this part of the calculation note that since there are 28 animals, any number higher than 28 should deduct 28 and any number higher than 56 which is 28 x 2, should deduct 56 from the total to reach a number that is lower than 28. This will indicate your Lunar Mansion number.

Once you have your number, which in this example is **2**, Your Sky Animal (or Lunar Mansion) is the one corresponding to the number 2 in Table 2 shown overleaf. In this example of someone born on 25th October 1974, your Sky Animal is the **Sky Dragon** and you belong to the Constellation of the **Green Dragon** of the Eastern skies. Your lucky day is **Friday** and you belong to the constellation season of **Spring**.

Meanwhile, based on your year of birth, you are born under the Zodiac sign of the **Wood Tiger**.

TABLE 1
To Determine the Animal of Your Day of Birth

MONTH	YEAR	YEAR	YEAR	YEAR	YEAR	NO.
-	1920*	1942	-	1987	2009	1
FEB, MAR	-	1943	1965	1988*	2010	2
-	1921	1944*	1966	-	2011	3
-	1922	-	1967	1989	2012*	4
APRIL	1923	1945	1968*	1990		5
-	1924*	1946	-	1991	2013	6
MAY	-	1947	1969	1992*	2014	7
-	1925	1948*	1970	-	2015	8
-	1926	-	1971	1993	2016*	9
JUNE	1927	1949	1972*	1994		10
-	1928*	1950		1995	2017	11
JULY	-	1951	1973	1996*	2018	12
-	1929	1952*	1974	-	2019	13
-	1930	-	1975	1997	2020*	14
AUGUST	1931	1953	1976*	1998		15
-	1932*	1954		1999	2021	16
-	-	1955	1977	2000*	2022	17
SEPTEMBER	1933	1956*	1978		2023	18
-	1934	-	1979	2001	2024*	19
OCTOBER	1935	1957	1980*	2002		20
-	1936*	1958		2003	2025	21
-	-	1959	1981	2004*	2026	22
NOVEMBER	1937	1960*	1982	-	2027	23
-	1938	-	1983	2005	2028*	24
DECEMBER	1939	1961	1984*	2006	-	25
-	1940*	1962		2007	2029	26
JANUARY	-	1963	1985	2008*	2030	27
-	1941	1964*	1986	-	2031	28

* indicates a leap year

TABLE 2
The 28 Animals of the Four Constellations

FAMILY OF THE GREEN DRAGON RULING THE SEASON OF SPRING	**FAMILY OF THE BLACK TORTOISE RULING THE SEASON OF WINTER**
Lunar Mansion Constellations of the **Eastern** skies	Lunar Mansion Constellations of the **Northern** skies
1. **Sky Salamander** THURSDAY	8. **Sky Unicorn** THURSDAY
2. **Sky Dragon** FRIDAY	9. **Sky Ox** FRIDAY
3. **Sky Beaver** SATURDAY	10. **Sky Bat** SATURDAY
4. **Sky Rabbit** SUNDAY	11. **Sky Rat** SUNDAY
5. **Sky Fox** MONDAY	12. **Sky Swallow** MONDAY
6. **Sky Tiger** TUESDAY	13. **Sky Boar** TUESDAY
7. **Sky Leopard** WEDNESDAY	14. **Sky Porcupine** WEDNESDAY

FAMILY OF THE WHITE TIGER RULING THE SEASON OF AUTUMN	**FAMILY OF THE CRIMSON PHOENIX RULING THE SEASON OF SUMMER**
Lunar Mansion Constellations of the **Western** skies	Lunar Mansion Constellations of the **Southern** skies
15. **Sky Wolf** THURSDAY	22. **Sky Ant Eater** THURSDAY
16. **Sky Dog** FRIDAY	23. **Sky Sheep** FRIDAY
17. **Sky Pheasant** SATURDAY	24. **Sky Antler** SATURDAY
18. **Sky Rooster** SUNDAY	25. **Sky Horse** SUNDAY
19. **Sky Raven** MONDAY	26. **Sky Deer** MONDAY
20. **Sky Monkey** TUESDAY	27. **Sky Snake** TUESDAY
21. **Sky Ape** WEDNESDAY	28. **Sky Worm** WEDNESDAY

Interacting With Others In 2011

Part 4

Tiger's Confidence & Winning Attitude Inspires

Many things affect how one animal sign gets along with another and the Chinese believe that much of this has to do with astrological forces and influences of a particular year. The varying factors result in a difference in compatibility levels each year and while it is impossible to take note of everything, the key variables to note are one's chi energy essence and whether the year's constellations are making you feel positive and good about yourself. The influence of the YEAR on the compatibilities of relationships is thus important; you cannot ignore the effect annual chi has on the way you interact with your loved ones and family.

New energies influence the way you treat people, in turn determining how they respond to you. Your interactions with close friends and loved ones are affected by your mental and physical state. So how you get on with your partner, your spouse, parents, children, siblings, relatives and friends are affected by your fortunes in any given year. These relationships create important inputs to your happiness.

Understanding compatibilities make you more understanding; so when differences crop up, these need not be taken to heart. Your good vibes make you tolerant but afflictive energies and negative stars suffered by others can make them seem rather tiresome.

Annual energy does influence the people you have greater or lesser affinity with. In some years, you might even feel an inexplicable aversion to someone you may always have liked and loved; or a sudden attraction to someone you previously found annoying! Usually, of course, the affinity groupings, secret friends alliances and ideal soul mate pairings of the Zodiac exert strong influences as well, but annual chi also has the power to sway your thinking and those of others. They can make you more argumentative or make you more loving. People tend to be more or less tolerant or selfish, cold or warm depending on the way things turn out for them from year to year. When life and work goes well, we become better disposed towards others. Then, even a natural zodiac enemy can become a soul mate, if only for a short period of time. Likewise, when one is being challenged by big problems, even the slightest provocation can lead to anger. Zodiac friends and allies might even then appear insufferable. A falling out between Horoscope allies is thus not impossible. In this section, we examine the Tiger's personal relationships with the other eleven signs in 2011.

In this section, we examine the Tiger's personal relationships with the other eleven signs in 2011.

Zodiac Influences

1. Alliance of Allies
2. Zodiac Soulmates
3. Secret Friends
4. Astrology Enemies
5. Peach Blossom
6. Seasonal Trinity

1. Alliance of Allies

Four affinity groupings of animal signs form an alliance of natural allies in the horoscope. The three signs possess similar thought processes, aspirations and goals. Their attitudes are alike, and their support of each other is usually instant and dependable.

All three signs having good fortune in any year makes the alliance strong, and if there is an alliance within a family unit as amongst siblings, or between spouses and a child, the family is extremely supportive, giving strength to each other. In good years, auspicious luck gets multiplied. Allies always get along. Any falling out is temporary. They trust each other and close ranks against external threats. Good astrological feng shui comes from carrying the image of your allies, especially when they are going through good years.

ALLY GROUPINGS	ANIMALS	CHARACTERISTICS
COMPETITORS	Rat, Dragon, Monkey	Competent, Tough, Resolute
INTELLECTUALS	Ox, Snake, Rooster	Generous, Focused, Resilient
ENTHUSIASTS	Dog, Tiger, Horse	Aggressive, Rebellious, Coy
DIPLOMATS	Boar, Sheep, Rabbit	Creative, Kind, Emotional

The Tiger and its allies together make up the numbers 1, 8, and 2 in the 2011 feng shui chart, which thus indicates that of the three, it is the Dog who is the luckiest. However, the Tiger also enjoys the luck of victory in 2011. It is the Horse that is afflicted by the illness star 2. Meanwhile, both the Tiger and Dog each also enjoy the one auspicious star of the 24 mountains each. So the strongest link in this alliance is the Dog, who has the number 8 star, but Tiger is also good. In 2011, this is a strong alliance. Tiger and Dog can carry the year for this Alliance.

Dog, Tiger and Horse as Allies of the Zodiac.

2. Zodiac Soulmates

There are six pairs of animal signs that create six Zodiac Houses of yin and yang soulmates. Each pair creates powerful bonding on a cosmic level. Marriages or business unions between people belonging to the same Zodiac House are extremely auspicious. In a marriage, there is promise of great happiness. In a commercial partnership, it promises much wealth and success. This pairing is also good between professional colleagues and siblings. The strength of each pair is different; with each having a defining strength with some making better commercial than marriage partners. How successful you are as a pair depends on how you bond. The table summarizes the key strength of each Zodiac house.

A coming together of Yang Tiger with its soul mate the Ying Rabbit creates the *House of Growth and Development*; it is not a strong alliance in 2011. The Rabbit is weak although the Tiger brings some great energy to the pairing. The Tiger here will take the initiative while the Rabbit tries to keep up and avoid getting in the way. Rabbit and Tiger work well together, so an alliance between them is beneficial, especially for the Rabbit. In this alliance, the Tiger benefits the Rabbit in 2011.

HOUSES OF PAIRED SOULMATES

ANIMALS	YIN/YANG	ZODIAC HOUSE OF CREATIVITY	TARGET UNLEASHED
Rat	YANG	HOUSE OF CREATIVITY & CLEVERNESS	The Rat initiates
Ox	YIN		The Ox completes
Tiger	YANG	HOUSE OF GROWTH & DEVELOPMENT	The Tiger employs force
Rabbit	YIN		The Rabbit uses diplomacy
Dragon	YANG	HOUSE OF MAGIC & SPRITITUALITY	The Dragon creates magic
Snake	YIN		The Snake creates mystery
Horse	YANG	HOUSE OF PASSION & SEXUALITY	The Horse embodies male energy
Sheep	YIN		The Sheep is the female energy
Monkey	YANG	HOUSE OF CAREER & COMMERCE	The Monkey creates strategy
Rooster	YIN		The Rooster gets things moving
Dog	YANG	HOUSE OF DOMESTICITY	The Dog works to provide
Boar	YIN		The Boar enjoys what is created

3. Secret Friends

There are six sets of a *secret friendship* that exists between the animal signs of the Zodiac. Between them a very powerful affinity exists making them excellent for each other. Love, respect and goodwill flow freely between secret friends; and they create wonderful happiness vibes for each other in a marriage. Once forged, it is a bond that is hard to break; and even when they themselves want to break, it will be hard for either party to fully walk away. This pair of signs will stick together through thick and thin.

In the pairing of secret friends the Tiger is paired with the Boar. There is a very special bond between these two animal signs as they are also Zodiac soulmates. In 2011 this is a very strong pair.

PAIRINGS OF SECRET FRIENDS

🐀	Rat	Ox	🐖
🐖	Boar	Tiger	🐅
🐕	Dog	Rabbit	🐇
🐉	Dragon	Rooster	🐓
🐍	Snake	Monkey	🐒
🐎	Horse	Sheep	🐐

4. Astrological Enemies

Then there are the astrological enemies of the Horoscope. This is the animal sign that directly confronts yours in the Astrology compass wheel. For the Ox, your enemy is the Sheep. Note that the enemy does not necessarily harm you; it only means someone of this sign can never be of any real help to you. But because both have the same intrinsic elements of Earth, Ox and Sheep can get on well under certain conditions.

PAIRINGS OF ASTROLOGICAL ENEMIES

🐀	Rat	Horse	🐴
🐖	Boar	Snake	🐍
🐕	Dog	Dragon	🐉
🐇	Rabbit	Rooster	🐓
🐅	Tiger	Monkey	🐒
🐂	Ox	Sheep	🐐

There is a six year gap between natural enemies. A marriage between them is not usually recommended. Thus marriage between a Tiger and a Monkey is better avoided unless other indications in their paht chee charts suggest otherwise. Nevertheless pairings between arrows of antagonism are generally discouraged. Tiger people are advised to refrain from getting involved with a Monkey over the long term, although on a year by year basis, this can sometimes be overcome by the energies of the particular year. But this is definitely not such a year.

As a business partnership, the pairing is likely to be problematic, and in the event of a split, the separation can be acrimonious even if they start out as best friends. In 2011 the Tiger and the Monkey will find themselves fighting non-stop if they are in business together.

5. Peach Blossom Links

Each of the Alliance of Allies has a special relationship with one of the four primary signs of Horse, Rat, Rooster and Rabbit in that these are the symbolic representations of love and romance for one Alliance group of animal signs. In the Horoscope, they are referred to as *peach blossom animals*, and the presence of their images in the homes of the matching Alliance of Allies brings peach blossom luck which is associated with love and romance.

The Tiger belongs to the Alliance of Tiger, Dog and Horse, which has the Rabbit as their peach blossom link. The Tiger will benefit from associating with anyone born in the Rabbit year, and will also benefit from placing a painting or image of a Rabbit in the East corner of the house, or in the Tiger direction of Northeast.

6. Seasonal Trinity

Another grouping of animal signs creates the four seasonal trinity combinations that bring the luck of seasonal abundance. To many astrology experts, this is regarded as one of the more powerful combinations, and when it exists within a family made up of either parent or both parents and with one or more children, it indicates that collectively, these family members are strong enough to transform all negative luck indications for the family members that make up the combination, for the entire year. The table below summarises the Seasonal groupings.

Thus when the annual indications of the year are not favourable, the existence of the seasonal combination of animal signs in any living abode can transform the bad luck into better luck especially during the season indicated by the combination. It is necessary for **all** three animal signs to live together in the *same house* or to be in the same office working in close proximity for this powerful pattern to work. For greater impact it is better feng shui if they are all using the direction

SEASONAL TRINITIES OF THE HOROSCOPE

ANIMAL SIGNS	SEASON	ELEMENT	DIRECTION
Dragon, Rabbit, Tiger	Spring	Wood	East
Snake, Horse, Sheep	Summer	Fire	South
Monkey, Rooster, Dog	Autumn	Metal	West
Ox, Rat, Boar	Winter	Water	North

associated with the relevant seasons. Thus the seasonal combination of Spring is East, while the seasonal combination of Summer is South.

The Tiger belongs to the combination of Spring, a combination which strengthens its links with the Dragon and the Rabbit. Should a Tiger and Dragon marry, and they have a Rabbit child for instance, the three will create the trinity of spring. With the trinity created, they attract the luck of abundance during the spring season!

TIGER WITH RAT

In 2011, Tiger soothes Rat's ruffled waters

This is a year when the Tiger becomes a pussycat, when it enjoys big time victory luck. And in its moments of triumph, the Tiger will soothe the flames of anger generated by an impatient, intolerant and bad-tempered Rat. This is not surprising since the Tiger is feeling strong in 2011 when the star numbers of the flying star chart as well as the 24 mountain constellation bring the stamp of heavenly approval. Cosmic energy for the Tiger blooms this year and there is both success and recognition. This is an unlikely pair because they really have very little in common. The aspirations of the big cat and the tiny mouse are at two ends of a long pole and yet when these two get together in 2011, there will be some good sparks generated.

Unlike the energies of the past year when the amorous Rat and the dour Tiger would have nothing binding them, in 2011, they find common ground and their level of vitality are at the same levels. Younger couples will be perkier and enjoy one another more, but even the older pairs of Tiger and Rat will find synergy and comfort in each other. In 2011, the Tiger's inner essence continues to be stronger than that of the Rat. This is excellent for the pair as it suggests that the Rat can take comfort in the Tiger's reassuring energy. In other words, anger and intolerance will not find fertile ground here.

In terms of their horoscope compatibility this year, the Rat and Tiger in their twenties have as good a time 2011 as they did last year and this is because both have high energy levels. The Fire Tiger could however tire out the Wood Rat. Jealousy and resentment can rear its ugly head should external distractions cause them to each stray out of their commitment to each other. Another danger to this pair is Rat's potentially explosive temper so it really is a case for staying cool.

For the 38 year old Water Rat and 36 year old Wood Tiger, if you are still together, the year brings happier times. Developments outside your relationship will happily conspire to bring you both a happier year. In this relationship, the Tiger tends to be too much under the thumb of the Rat, mainly because Rat's Water energy puts it at an advantage. Here, the Rat must be determined to make things work, otherwise, perhaps there could be an amicable split. For the 51 year old Metal Rat and 48 year old Water Tiger, the strength in the relationship lies with the Tiger who is at an advantage. But with good destiny luck facing both of you, 2011 should turn out to be more harmonious than stressful.

TIGER WITH OX
Tiger's strength benefits Ox this year

The Ox and Tiger both possess strong temperaments and can be quite unbending when it comes to their principles and belief systems. Both also have a tendency to be stubborn in any disagreement that may arise between them. As a couple, therefore these are two people who must have some basic respect and high regard for one another, then only can they live harmoniously with each other. When these attributes define their relationship, they will be able in 2011 to take their relationship to a higher level. If they do not, then Ox could leave Tiger behind and go it alone. This arises from Tiger being afflicted on its left flank where the five yellow could cause it to stumble and fall.

The problem in this pairing is that both signs tend to be proud; neither the Ox nor the Tiger are the sort to swallow their self-cherishing "dignity" and apologise, or to ask for help or to even explain. These are characters that go into a stubborn silence whenever problems arise. To alleviate this, they should have a common goal, a shared passion upon which to direct their energies - if they do have this, then this is a couple that will enjoy the year. The Ox will benefit from the Tiger's strength, while the Tiger can absorb some of the Ox's great celestial good fortune.

In 2011, the Ox is definitely on a roll, but then so is the Tiger. This is a year when both are not especially focused on romance. This works out well as work opportunities distract the Ox, and intermittent blockages in the Tiger's professional life will keep it busy and occupied. This serves well the couple already married. The Tiger already hitched to an Ox will be tolerant rather than antagonistic, but there is not much in terms of romantic sparks between them. They are not at their best in the relationship. In 2011, the constellations favor the Ox in terms of luck, but the Tiger is stronger in terms of energy and chi essence.

Those in a dating situation will find themselves paying less attention to the romantic side of their relationship and focus more on whether or not they are compatible in their working relationship. In 2011, the Ox and Tiger in their twenties tend to have similar aspirations but different viewpoints on how to achieve what they both want. The good news is that theirs is a productive kind of relationship as their heavenly stems are complementary to each other with the Tiger's Fire stem feeding the older Ox's Wood stem. As for the Ox/Tiger pairing in their thirties, the Water Ox will be more tolerant of the Wood Tiger, but it is not the best of relationships because both will get distracted easily.

TIGER WITH TIGER
Inspiring one another to win big

The Tiger is a bundle of high energy expectations in 2011. As a pair, these big cats inspire one another as if their auras were touched by heaven, and as if the cosmic energies around them spark some inner fire. Gone is the listlessness of the previous year and in its place, we see a new view of the world. This reflects the wonderful effect of the Heaven Seal star which has flown directly into their astrological compass location. This star brings powerful invigorating chi energy which helps Tiger brush aside the negative influences of the side five yellow and instead encourage it to reach for the fulfilment of the big auspicious star on its right side.

Two Tigers together also reflect the presence of the Tigers in the year's paht chee chart. So this will likely turn out to be a year when unexpected deviations professionally and work wise bring new opportunities. There is a new exhilaration that will thrill the Tiger and send some sparks flying as well. The Tiger and its mate will seek new ways to make the best of the year because somehow the pervasive attitude in this relationship has turned happily positive. They enthusiastically embrace the new energy, believing the impossible to now become enticingly possible.

This is the effect of receiving the heavenly seal of high anticipation.

The 49 year old Water Tiger has much to look forward to this year, so for a pair of Water Tigers, life takes on rosier hues, which include excellent financial gains. Water Tigers enjoy a very good year filled with prosperity-bringing opportunities. The other lucky Tiger pairing will be between two 25 year old Fire Tigers whose vigor exceeds all other Tigers. Health luck is super in 2011 and this means there is strength and the best kind of attitude to go in search of new directions and opportunities. With good horoscope and feng shui chart indications, they are likely to find exciting success.

Tigers have a tendency to be snobbish and insensitive, and in years when this aspect of their attributes makes them insufferable to others, few will gravitate to the Tiger personality. But 2011 is quite the opposite. Blessed by heaven and enjoying the Victory Star of 1, Tigers in 2011 are surprisingly charming and engaging, not snobbish at all. Hence in 2011 they interact well with their own signs and with many others. But do not expect Tigers to change their stripes, not for anyone, so they bond better with their own kind than with others.

TIGER WITH RABBIT
Big cat holding hands with small hare

Tiger and Rabbit rarely ignore one another on first meeting. They have something special that breathes life into their relationship. We see an instant warming to each other and in 2011, empathy develops quickly. It is just like last year, except in this year, the Tiger is the one who gets drawn to the Rabbit in distress. Tiger quickly observes that Rabbit has to cope with some mortal blows brought by feng shui afflictions, and it touches something deep inside its chest. The big cat feels empathy rising.

The year of the Rabbit brings the strong presence of afflictive stars in the sign's compass location. This might put off those who sense the smell of Rabbit's discomfort and shy away, but not the Tiger. The big cat responds positively and becomes a shoulder and a good friend, pumping new energy by sheer force of friendship and love. It takes them no time at all to develop something serious between them irrespective of who is taking the initiative and who is responding. Like last year, both Rabbit and Tiger make appearances in the 2011 paht chee chart and this enhances their contemporary energy chi. Tiger appears twice and is next to the Rabbit, just like last year. This indicates auspiciousness for these two people coming together. They develop a closeness quickly; their attitudes and opinions resonate easily off each other as they bounce ideas and exchange confidences. It does not matter about the gender; the attraction between these two signs is obvious and even electric! They will mirror each other's tastes and attitudes, finding common ground at different levels, spiritually as well as intellectually. Their astrological perspectives cause them to work and play to the same rhythm. This has its source in their strong connection to the Season of Spring, which highlights the renewal of things and because they are intrinsically Wood element people, hence mindful of the vital ingredients needed in the growth process.

If they go into business together, it is easy for them to blend their skills in a seamless way with minimal friction, conducive to achieving the most productive results. Their methods may not be the same, but as a team, they are effective. They benefit from Dragon energy, so having a Dragon child or enhancing their space with a Dragon image benefits them. Two sets of pairings - the 49 year old Water Tiger and 48 year old Water Rabbit, as well as the 25 year old Fire Tiger/24 year old Fire Rabbit - continue on a roll through 2011 as they experience prosperity and growth despite new obstacles. Together they successfully create the *House of Growth and Development* for their families.

TIGER WITH DRAGON
Unlikely comrades forge beneficial alliance

The Tiger has always been the cosmic alter ego of the Dragon. These two animals are part of the celestial constellations of heaven, and on earth, they are also the celestial guardians of the East and West of the feng shui land compass. They are either comrades or foes depending on the feng shui winds of a particular year or period, although in the fresh new season of Spring, the Tiger and Dragon always work together as cosmic comrades, with the Dragon bringing the rain and the Tiger acting as a catalyst for the sun to shine.

In 2011, both the Tiger and Dragon are touched by heaven energy. The Tiger sits on heaven's seal while the Dragon is refreshed by the heavenly winds. In the feng shui chart, the number of heaven flies into Dragon's location. This is thus a year when they become unlikely comrades. It is a year when any alliance they forge will bring benefits to both. It is thus a great year for a Tiger and Dragon marriage or of either sign coming together with the other. These two signs will rise to prominence in the time of Spring, for that is when the rain falls and the world is instantly carpeted with new growth. The Tiger/Dragon union will enjoy a burst of good fortune, especially so if they are able to surround themselves with the all powerful Water element. This will let them connect at a deeper level. In 2011 they must avoid parched places, countries suffering from droughts or excessive dry spells.

The vitality of the Dragon and Tiger finds expression in the way they work as a team, attracting people of influence and power into their space. Heaven luck always brings mentor luck, so the year brings assistance and the goodwill of high-ranking helpful people into the lives of this pair. This suggests transformational energies that open new pathways. It is all very exciting indeed, enough to keep them on a high.

The Dragon and Tiger are strong and determined individuals, so as a partnership, they are able to transform opportunities into successful new ventures. The only risk they have is that of one being too strong for the other. In 2011 they must be mindful of the intensity of their work ethics. Being strongly motivated is well and good, but there must also be room for occasional rest and slow-down. It is not necessary to rush at the expense of being careless. The year is not without its hurdles and requires care to avoid the pitfalls. Having said that, note that for the Tiger and Dragon, this is a good year to move forward, and to set your ambitious dreams of success into motion.

TIGER WITH SNAKE
Strength in good teamwork

In 2011, the Tiger will be inexplicably drawn to the Snake, mesmerized by the easy confidence and stylish posture of this fire sign. The Snake is enjoying another great year and its aura is so strong it evokes admiration from the Tiger, where before, just a year ago, there was envy and even a latent resentment. This year, antipathy changes to awe, and for some, it can even become a fixation.

The Snake in 2011 exudes a self-assured and trendy personality that many find enticing, and the Tiger simply cannot resist. It is just as well that in 2011, the Snake who is single and available is open to propositions, and thus will not be averse to any overtures made by the Tiger. In fact, it is possible that the Tiger's own self assurance will make the Snake take notice.

A pairing of these two signs manifests heaven's magic and it will be a wonderful time for them in 2011. There is much happiness indicated arising from the feng shui winds affecting them both. As a couple, they will cause some good benefits to emerge. There is good team work between them, excellent mindfulness to their commitment to each other and cooperation - all of which suggest they can work together. Tiger is able to identify with Snake's enthusiasm for life, and both experience an exhilaration that reflects Snake's inner energy. The Snake puts many signs to shame this year (without doing anything other than being itself) and it is easy for just about anyone to feel comparatively inadequate, if one allows comparisons to cloud a relationship with this sign.

The Tiger thankfully is feeling a lot stronger and so is able to relate to the Snake at a transformative level. It is like heaven working its magic on the Tiger and Snake pair, bringing joyousness to a challenging and stimulating relationship. The Snake happily responds to Tiger's overtures.

Those of you already married to each other will find that 2011 brings a renewal of past attraction that brings a new phase to your relationship. Last year was not good, but this year, Tiger and Snake can rekindle a trust that had been missing for some time.

The improved sentiments come from both signs being affected by the good influence of heaven energy; plus this year, their feng shui chart numbers are extremely compatible and auspicious as well. This augurs well for them both.

TIGER WITH HORSE
Bringing out the best in each other

The Tiger and its astrological ally, the Horse continue to find companionship together, bringing out all that is good and noble in each other. These are two of the Zodiac's more unpredictable signs, yet with each other, it seems like they are able to read each other's mind; this shows how in sync they are. The Tiger is very simpatico with the Horse. They enjoy the same kind of interests and have a similar sense of humor, sharing a love for fast cars and adventure trails for instance. The Tiger and Horse tend to be more outdoor than indoor people, and they feel at home hiking up mountains or scaling the heights of some steep cliff face. They have a high threshold of endurance and enjoy the hunt. If brought together in a love relationship, they really can and will have a wild dance.

For these two, their love transcends physical attraction! Very much present is a profound and almost mystical connection which takes them both to heights of joyousness. They really make each other happy. In 2011, Tiger looks to Horse for inspiration and encouragement and when there is victory (and there are several in 2011) the Tiger who has a Horse to share the moment with, will find the victorious moments a lot more meaningful. In the year of the Rabbit, the Horse is not in a strong place, being afflicted by the illness star and suffering under the influence of the *Reducing Energy* star. Tiger on the other hand is stronger with no afflictions to disturb or distract. So in 2011 it is the Tiger who provides the comforting shoulders.

Last year, Tiger lacked the vitality of this current year, so those of you married to each other will find yourselves closer than ever because of Horse's great supportive nature last year when Tiger went through a troubled times. The Tiger in 2011 possesses a strong and powerful awareness of what needs to be done to make the most of the year. The Tiger knows there are good opportunities awaiting them as a pair, and thus will be the catalyst getting them both inspired. Communication between them will be intuitive; thus all that more powerful and they will have fun pursuing dreams and ambitions.

Note that the Tiger and Horse belong to the Alliance that includes the loyal Dog. Together they are the "three hunters" of the Chinese Zodiac. Their patience and skill in "smelling" out good deals are legendary; this year, the qualities of this pair will lift them high, helping them attain heights of triumphant moments. With the Horse by its side, the Tiger will be inspired to aim high, think big and win.

TIGER WITH SHEEP
Heaven & earth chi bring them together

In 2011, the Tiger discovers qualities in the Sheep it was previously blind to. There are cosmic connections between these two signs; a powerful yin and yang type bonding that manifests heaven and earth influences. This acts like a magnet for this pair, drawing them close in spite of whatever differences or reservations they may each have.

Those married to each other will find the fires get lit again by cosmic connections. It is a good year for them as a couple; this is a year when they find themselves strongly motivated by each other. This can be a most powerful aphrodisiac.

It is uncanny to see the Tiger and Sheep cavorting together lost in one another's presence and actually finding joy being in each other's company, when in most years these are signs that would ordinarily have little interest in each other.

They do not have much in common; their interests could not be further apart and personality-wise they do not even enjoy complementary skills or attitudes. There is little that could be the basis for a rock solid relationship. Yet in 2011, real love and affection sparks up between the Tiger and Sheep, fuelled principally by the Sheep's peach blossom star influence. In the light of this powerful star, and given Tiger's heaven seal connecting with Sheep's earth seal, these two signs will be blind to anything other than the attraction and respect they inspire in each other.

In 2011 this will be an emotional relationship; it will have little to do with the head or any careful thinking. The Tiger person will find the Sheep's conservative nature quaint, even attractive. The Sheep on the other hand finds passion with the Tiger.

Should these two signs be married, it is likely that the Tiger will be older than the Sheep and this works well. A match between the 61 year old Tiger would work well with the 32 year old Earth Sheep or the 49 year old Water Tiger might go for the 20 year old Metal Sheep. This has to do with the elements, with the Sheep element "producing" the Tiger element! All other age pairings work as well because the winds that blow to them are so complementary and in harmony.

Both the Tiger and Sheep are up to being amiable or sociable this year. They are in a loving mood so there will be no confrontations to spoil the pretty picture they make.

TIGER WITH MONKEY
This pairing could lead to scandal

The Tiger and Monkey are astrological adversaries who bristle with cool antagonism each time they meet. Their energies are mutually destructive, usually with the Monkey annoying the Tiger. It is unlikely that any pairing between these two can be harmonious or loving for very long. In 2011 however, the scenario appears conducive to them pushing aside differences and living through some kind of truce should they be married; but for those not married to one another, any coming together smells of some kind of illicit liaison.

In 2011, Tiger's sense of self preservation is tempered by the *Heaven Seal* star hovering within its cosmic auric field, making it susceptible to romantic overtures; Monkey meanwhile is affected by the *Peach Blossom* star which fills its head with thoughts of love and romance. The chi energy favors them coming together should they meet. They are attracted to one another, but it will be a romance unlikely to run smooth.

The Tiger and Monkey are not softies. Both are signs that forge headlong into relationships, often throwing caution to the winds. They push past boundaries of decorum with scant regard for the niceties; so it is not impossible that in getting together, they cause longer term problems for themselves. In 2011, the Monkey sign continues to be hard-headed, except now its romantic inclinations rise to the fore, taking centre stage in its priorities. Monkey feels love and lust and passion. Water and Fire Monkey people are unbeatable and for Tiger to get involved with either of these two Monkeys is really asking for trouble, even though the big cat here is not exactly helpless.

The feng shui chart suggests that a combination of their energies in 2011 can be harmful to both sides. It will be to Tiger's advantage to let sensible notions of propriety prevail over Monkey's passion. It is better not to succumb to whatever feelings are kindled by the charming Monkey, who in 2011 takes on the role of cad to the Tiger. Be careful. The Tiger would do well to remember that the Monkey is its mortal enemy in the Zodiac scheme of things. Monkey's Metal element cuts through Monkey's Wood element. The element relationship itself is thus destructive, and best avoided.

However, in 2011, there is the possibility that underlying currents between Tiger and Monkey may prove too strong and so override common sense. The line between love and hate is a fine one. At the heart of passion however lie seeds of eventual destruction.

TIGER WITH ROOSTER
Better to stay clear of each other

In 2011, Tiger the cat is in for a triumphant year while the Rooster, the bird is afflicted and has its hands full coping with the direct onslaught of the Tai Sui, as well as the powerful negative energies brought by the 24 mountain stars constellation. It is an uneven match in 2011, one that does not favor the Rooster and being the smart bird that it is, Rooster runs far from Tiger.

Against the heaven sent posture of the Tiger, Rooster cleverly flies away to avoid falling into danger. These two signs are not enemies but they are also not friends. Rooster's Metal element is viewed as a threat by the Tiger whose element is Wood. There is an underlying suspicion that will prevent this pair from ever fully trusting one another. In 2011, the Tiger is concerned about moving ahead; and ambition rears its mighty head. It will view the Rooster with total detachment.

There simply cannot be anything very deep developing between these two signs and for those of you just meeting up and connecting, it is far better to let things remain casual between you. Getting too involved with one another will not do either of you much good. The Rooster is too cocky to be motivated by Tiger and the Tiger cannot see much to respect in the Rooster.

Between these two signs there will always be concerns related to their egos and their *"face"*. Pride is important to them both. It plays a big part of their relationship interface. So any relationship started between them could sink into painful tension. Competitive tendencies intrude into their relationship and this is where there can be unhappiness for both.

Neither the Tiger nor Rooster are known for their tolerance, being impatient and quick to temper. In other years they might come together and forge an alliance against the odds, but in 2011, the Rooster is feeling deflated, recognising the weakness of its position, and thus will divert its life force and inner strengths to battling the effects of the three killings and the wrath of the Tai Sui.

If a Tiger is married to a Rooster, it is also best to leave Rooster well alone to handle its own tribulations. In 2011, the Tiger benefits from the Star of Victory, which brings triumphant moments. This has a bearing on their respective roles in any Tiger/Rooster marriage. Both being strong-willed, it is better not to stand in each other's way. So to ensure a smooth year for both, each should just leave the other well alone.

TIGER WITH DOG
Amazing pair and very auspicious too

The year 2011 is a great year for these two allies of the Zodiac. This is when good things come equally big and as powerful to both signs of the Tiger and the Dog; and the great news is that yes you will both stay true to one another. The Tiger and Dog continue to be good for each other and also continue to need each other.

The Tiger's affections for the sign of the Dog arises as much from the Dog's dependability as a soul mate as from Dog's steadfastness and loyalty. These sentiments are likewise reciprocated by the Dog, so this is a couple who can work in tandem to manifest the excellent indications in their horoscope and their respective feng shui chart locations.

Their allegiance to one another brings excellent results in what looks to be a really excellent year for both.

The Tiger and Dog are lucky this year. The Tiger enjoys the luck of victory, while the Dog will feel the auspicious luck of the number 8 flying into its location. True, the Dog continues to have a low level indication for its life force and inner essence, but the power of 8 more than makes up for this. Those married to one another will find that simply standing together in 2011 will bring them good fortune. The two signs' numbers in the feng shui chart enjoy what we refer to as the white numbers combination – these are the numbers 1 and 8 which indicate that together the strength of the white numbers get doubled. It is possible that this pair can develop and grow something truly meaningful between them.

The Tiger and Dog are usually great for each other irrespective of what the year brings. They bring out the best in one another and there is genuine love and understanding flowing between them. There are also no competitive issues or pressures that can be so strong as to burst their happiness bubble.

They make friends easily and can work well in business together; indeed it is likely that they start out as work colleagues then becoming lifelong partners.

The good news for this well-matched pair is that 2011 promises to be excellent for them to build something together. They can move ahead with confidence; reach for the skies and climb as high as they want to. Indeed, having each other to share the climb and the high of victories is what will make their lives meaningful. This is the essence of happiness, and what makes something well worth pursuing.

TIGER WITH BOAR
An excellent combination

The Tiger will have great relationship potential with the Boar this coming year, and should you hook up with someone from this sign in 2011, the rewards are many and the happiness is lovely indeed. The Tiger will derive great satisfaction from any kind of friendship of love relationship with the Boar.

2011 will be a year when Boar's positive chi energy lifts you high, making you feel that anything at all is positive. So it is a motivating relationship that chugs along through a year when whatever troubles or disasters may be on the horizon are somehow deflected. Tiger's *Heaven Seal* creates a veneer of protective energy so that your focus will be on the daily things that make you happy rather than whatever problems may be in the larger picture of the world stage.

In many ways, this is the same for the Boar, although focus for the Boar is on making good things happen at the work front. The Boar is energized by the power of 8 star as well as by the auspicious stars of the 24 mountain constellation bringing the promise of financially great things looming on the near horizon. These two signs are of course secret friends of the

Zodiac, and in 2011, they enjoy the added benefits of having their feng shui numbers create the all-powerful and auspicious white star numbers combination. In the feng shui chart, Tiger is 1 and Boar is 8, and 1/8 are both very lucky white stars, which bring with them the energy of victory, success and good fortune.

The Tiger and Boar are extremely compatible. Irrespective of the variations of their chi energy from year to year, they are one of the more successful pairings of the astrological Zodiac, sharing similar aspirations and motivated by the same issues. They are positive people who have a calmness of purpose, and they rarely get upset when times get challenging. In good years, they take everything good that comes in their stride enjoying their good fortune silently and with little fanfare.

As a couple, these two signs are naturally supportive of each other. They are rarely, if ever, disloyal, and they see only the good side of one another. For them, marriage is a serious commitment, as is their allegiance to each other. So this is a couple that will rarely be beset by problems of infidelity. The Tiger especially is always mindful of its obligations, pledges and promises made to this love relationship.

Ox's Monthly Horoscope 2011

Part 5

Good Timing Helps You Actualize Big Auspicious Luck!

Your luck improves considerably this year compared to the year just past. This is a year characterized by growth and new opportunities for the Tiger person. You will see significant improvements in your life. Barriers and blockages to success disintegrate, leaving you a blank canvas with which to paint your dreams. You also enjoy Big Auspicious luck, while potential for achieving great things is there, you must also contend with the Side Five Yellow affliction. Success potential is most definitely there, but what you must remember this year is that success cannot be achieved alone.

1 ST MONTH
February 4th - March 5th 2011

COULD GET SICK EASILY SO BE CAREFUL

There is danger of falling ill or hurting yourself in careless accidents this month. It is thus important to be extra cautious when it comes to your health and safety over the next few weeks. Physical injuries such as pulled muscles and bruises may befall you. Avoid taking risks when it comes to dangerous sports. This is not a good month to "*rough it out*" as physically you are vulnerable at this time. Negative aspects aside, this month puts you in a very influential position in your own social and professional circles. Others seek your opinion on important issues, and act on your advice when you give it. However, do not let this overinflate your ego.

WORK & CAREER - *Work with Others*

Because of your lower energy levels this month, you may be tempted to rush things at work to complete your tasks quickly. But be careful not to compromise the quality of your work. If you have deadlines you're finding difficult to meet, discuss this with your boss rather than producing substandard work. Sometimes bringing work home with you can help your output levels. Avoid staying late at the office night after night. Learn to plan your schedule and set yourself interim deadlines to help you. This month especially you benefit from working closer with your colleagues and co-workers. Learn to work well with others and you'll turn out the results you're looking efficiently and without undue stress.

BUSINESS – *Opportunity to Expand*

For the Tiger in business, you could meet with an opportunity to expand your business in some new directions, and you will certainly benefit from partners with influence and power in high places. If the joint venture makes sense, there is no reason why you shouldn't go ahead. Just try not to enter a partnership that's lopsided where you have to do all the work. If one side is putting in more time, resources, money and effort, there's likely to be a fall-out sometime in the not so distant future. Before jumping into anything, consider all eventualities carefully. Make plans now, but leave the signing of any agreements or documentation till next month.

LOVE & RELATIONSHIPS – *Head not Heart*

Tigers already in steady relationships may have to adopt a take-charge attitude with their partners this month. There may be less happening in the bedroom due to your weakened physical health and lack of energy, but there is deep fulfillment to be had at a more intellectual level. Conversations become more stimulating, so make an effort to communicate more. For the single Tiger, chances are good for you to meet someone at social occasions linked to your work. You could meet someone of real interest this month, but if you're looking to "go steady", it is far better to wait till next month, when your luck is better on this front.

HEALTH & WELLNESS – *Pace Yourself*

You're afflicted by the illness star this month, making you more susceptible to catching all kinds of bugs. Avoid living it up this month. Pace yourself or you could feel the ill effects very quickly. Elderly Tiger people should avoid sleeping in the Northeast sector this month, and should wear a Wu Lou health gourd in gold. Also place a metal one next to your bed where you sleep. This will help control the illness vibes that threaten to play havoc with your life.

EDUCATION – *Make Time to Unwind*

This could be a taxing month for the young Tiger in school. Things are hectic and if you leave a piece of work too long, you could see your work pile building up. Try to complete assignments quite soon after they are set to avoid stressing yourself out unnecessarily. Then make some time for rest and relaxation, or for indulging in a favorite hobby.

2ND MONTH
March 6th - April 4th 2011

WINNING ENERGY DOUBLES

This is a fabulous month for the Tiger when you have Victory Luck doubled. You do well in any competitive situation you find yourself in and bask in triumph and success. Don't go for shallow victories. This is a time when you can make meaningful achievements in your life. The month is also characterized by change, so be prepared to go through a possible significant transformation. Your luck is auspicious during this time, so changes experienced will be positive and beneficial. Those with lofty ambitions can expect to fly high and unimpeded. Be brave this month. You have the backing of Lady Luck. Carry the **Victory Banner** amulet to enhance your special kind of luck this month.

WORK & CAREER - *Think Things Through*

Expect to meet with some sizeable changes when it comes to your career this month. Some of these may be thrust upon you, others caused by you whether directly or indirectly. For some of you, your thought processes could be turning towards a change in direction, attitude or even a change in job. Before you make any huge leaps of faith, think things through carefully. You can afford to be brave, but not foolhardy. While you enjoy your fair share of good luck this year, there are also some minefields to dodge. Those of you who live by your intelligence, making sound decisions that are thought through and not merely "*from the heart*" are likely to enjoy a significant advantage.

BUSINESS - *Knowledge is All Important*

A good month for the Tiger-born in business. You can invest and expand without worry this month. You do not need to worry so much about your financial situation, leaving you room to think about growing new markets and capturing more market share. Study industry trends and spend time on analysis. While going with your instincts works well for you, you can further hone those instincts to a fine art by having more background information. Knowledge is an important ally this month. Talk to people and make the most of your networking. Even inconsequential pieces of information could prove useful. You never know when your next big tip will be coming, or where you will be getting it from, but as long as you stay alert, it will dawn on you when you are about to hit something big.

LOVE & RELATIONSHIPS - *Big Picture*

Your love life is fulfilling because suddenly certain things become crystal clear to you. If you are in a partnership that's no longer working, your eyes will open up to that fact. Or if you have been taking your partner for granted, you will realize what a gem you have and start to nurture your relationship, becoming more generous and giving. To help make good decisions when it comes to matters of the heart, wear a mystic knot to guide you in your choices. Change is good this month, but when making decisions, do not take a self-centered approach. Decisions taken now are likely to be long lasting, so make sure you make the right ones by looking at the big picture.

EDUCATION - *Rich & Diverse*

Your school career will be rich and diverse this month, and you happily have all the energy you need to make the most of it. Because school work is going well, this also leaves you enough free time to pursue your other interests with gusto.

3RD MONTH
April 5th - May 5th 2011

SUM-OF-TEN BRINGS CONTINUOUS SUCCESS

What a fabulous month for the Tiger person. Completion luck brings you much joy; projects and undertakings started months ago start to gel and come together. There is a bright light at the end of the tunnel and your intended path becomes clearer than ever. It is a fast paced month, but one you will enjoy tremendously if you let yourself. Wealth and income luck is good, and you see advances made in your career.

For the romantic Tiger, there is plenty of passion to be had! Be bold and valiant in your conquests! Savor every moment this month and don't let the small things weigh you down. If you find yourself worrying about the little things, step back and study your lot. You'll realize there's a lot more to smile than frown about!

WORK & CAREER – *Going Places*

It's a busy time at work, but this brand of busy is extremely palatable. You see yourself going places, with your career path neatly mapped out for you.

You're well appreciated by your superiors and your co-workers, and you start to truly enjoy what you do. There may be a lot heaped on your plate but as long as you spend a few moments each day taking stock, you'll be well on top of everything. Networking brings benefits. This is a time when you can afford to take a higher profile. Make your presence felt. Tiger people enjoy the attention, so use it to your benefit this month. Your creativity levels are high and you have a lot to contribute. If you've been akin to just taking orders, this is a good time to show you can offer a whole lot more. Be more forceful when trying to impress someone, and they are bound to sit up and take notice.

BUSINESS - *Look to the Big Prize*

The hard work you have been putting in start to translate into results, and this can happen suddenly and out of the blue. Celebrate and take pride in your efforts, but also keep looking forward to the next step. You are on a roll and it would be a great shame to stop when there's so much more you can achieve. Don't allow yourself to be satisfied with interim successes. Look to the big prize, because it's there for the taking for those of you who want it. Contacts made in the past prove useful this month. Spend more of your effort networking. Even if help does not come directly, regular contact with the right people could enlighten you to some valuable information that can steer you in the right direction.

LOVE & RELATIONSHIPS - *Blissful*

Dreams and desires are well within your reach this month! Whether you're looking to start a serious relationship or are out for some harmless fun, you can have it any way you want! Single Tigers enjoy flattering attention from various admirers and someone particularly appealing could step into your life in the next few weeks. It is a highly romantic time to get hitched, so those of you who are looking for the right time to tie the knot, this is as good a time as any. Married Tigers will find this an opportune time to rekindle the old flames of romance. Don't let a busy work schedule cramp your love life. When there's a will there's a way. And this month, a strong will will pay off handsomely!

EDUCATION - *Center of Attention*

Your energy levels are up and there is so much you can achieve! You're likely the center of attention in your social circle and enjoying every minute of it! Some of the more wayward of you young Tigers may find it difficult to focus on studies when there's so much happening, but as long as you schedule your time well, you will be able to cope.

4TH MONTH
May 6th – June 5th 2011

ANOTHER SUPERB MONTH TO GO FORWARD

What a fabulous month for the Tiger-born. The next few weeks will see good luck searching you out! Little will go wrong for you, so this is the time to make the most of your good fortune.

This is a good month to plan all your important signings, meetings, launches and anything else of significance. Wealth and money luck is also good this month. Activate wealth luck to ensure you make the most of the good starts in your chart this month. Display a **wealth ship** sailing into your home from an auspicious direction and each day this month, add a small treasure to your ship. Treasures can be gold bars, golden ingots, real cash or jewels and gemstones. Love luck is also extremely promising this month.

Display a wealth ship sailing into your home from an auspicious direction.

WORK & CAREER - *A Productive Time*

Work is particularly exciting this month. You will find yourself extremely productive at work and completing tasks well and on time comes easily. In fact, you may seem to get things finished more quickly than required. This is a great month to look ahead at your career path before you. For some of you, it will be a time when you leapfrog onto a new level. Start taking on more difficult tasks and applying yourself more. Make sure you stay on the good side of your boss by being totally dependable. You may have to cover for a colleague at some point and if it doesn't harm you, do so. It is useful to gain loyal allies at work.

BUSINESS - *An Extremely Auspicious Time*

This is a good time to start new projects, sign agreements, enter into a promising joint venture or launch a new product. It is also a fruitful time to engage in important discussions, as these are likely to go your way. Your fortunes are looking good, and others will be attracted to your good Chi. If you need to approach someone for a favor, or with a proposal, do so this month. Schedule important meetings during times that are auspicious for you. You can pick your dates and times based on the Feng Shui Almanac. But your luck is so good right now you needn't worry too much.

LOVE - *Lose Your Inhibitions*

This is a romantic month for the Tiger. If you're single and hoping to meet a prospective partner, smarten up and dress a little better this month. Making the extra effort will ensure you get your fair share of suitors. Accept invitations to parties and events. Even a blind date set up by a friend could be quite fun. Lose your inhibitions if you really want to enjoy yourself and who knows, you may just find someone you can really build a future with. Be a bit wild and hold on tight for the ride. The month has plenty of good things in store for you, which you'll never see if you don't let yourself. For married Tigers, this is a good opportunity to focus extra attention on your marriage. If you make an effort, the rewards will be more than worthwhile.

EDUCATION - *Smooth*

Things go smoothly for the young Tiger. You are full of self-confidence and if you apply yourself with good motivation and effort, things will go extremely well. If you are sitting exams this month, rest easy that luck is on your side. As long as you've put in the study hours, you will have little to worry about.

5TH MONTH
June 6th - July 6th 2011

CARELESSNESS COULD CAUSE PROBLEMS

This could be a stressful month at work. Colleagues you thought were on your side could betray you or let you down, whether intentionally or otherwise. This is a time when it is every man for himself. Don't leave yourself vulnerable to criticism. You need to step carefully this month for there could be challengers at the workplace who stand to gain from your loss. Small mistakes made on your part could be blown out of proportion. Avoid making careless slip-ups by being meticulous with your work. Don't let yourself get too tired and be sure to have some time to refresh and recharge. Fatigue could prove costly.

WORK & CAREER - *Step Carefully*

This could be a stressful month at work. Colleagues you thought were on your side could betray you or let you down, whether intentionally or otherwise. This is a time when it is every man for himself. Don't leave yourself vulnerable to criticism. You need to step carefully this month for there could be challengers at the workplace who stand to gain from your loss. Small mistakes made on your part could be blown out of proportion. Avoid making careless slip-ups by being meticulous with your work. Don't let yourself get too tired and be sure to have some time to refresh and recharge; fatigue could prove costly.

BUSINESS - *Avoid Taking Financial Risks*

Better to lie low and avoid doing too much this month. Don't try to interfere with the systems too much. If everything is bowling along nicely, leave it be. Stay out of internal politics among your staff. Trying to play the part of mediator will fall flat, so it is best to let personality problems sort themselves out. Customers and clients may have more complaints than usual this month, but you're probably not the best person to deal with this. Let your staff handle them if you're feeling particularly prickly. Avoid engaging in confrontations as you have the potential to blow up, with damaging consequences. Calm your temper by avoiding situations that make your blood boil. Avoid taking financial risks and watch your cash flow carefully. Not a good time to sign on new deals or to go into new partnerships. Wait till your luck improves next month.

LOVE & RELATIONSHIPS - *Be Careful*

Not an agreeable time for the Tiger and this could show up when it comes to your relationships. Disagreements and quarrels between you and your spouse are likely, especially if you let yourself get aggravated at the slightest things. If you're single, this is probably not the best time to pursue a new relationship, as you could end up showing off your flaws rather than your qualities. Some Tigers could also find themselves attracting the wrong kind of suitor. Lady Tigers should be careful of the bad boys out there. If you're married, it is a good idea to protect your marriage by being more understanding. Your temper and disposition if not kept in check could drive your partner into the arms of someone else. Avoid opening up your marriage to temptation and keep your wits about you this month. Wear a **Rooster and Amethyst and Fan** to guard against external romance.

EDUCATION - *Distracted*

For the young Tiger, things could get unpleasant if there is a power struggle between you and a peer. Resist the urge to hurl back abuse thrown your way. Let it slide and keep the month peaceful. You may be distracted from schoolwork and find it difficult to concentrate in class. Leave your troubles behind and sort them out later. For now, try and focus.

6TH MONTH
July 7th - Aug 7th 2011

GOOD HEAVEN ENERGY
BRINGS MENTOR LUCK

Luck is on your side, bringing new opportunities in work and love. Things go magnificently this month and improve a hundred fold from the month just past. This is a favorable time for you to get ahead when it comes to your career, so make the most of it by seizing opportunities that come your way. Take the advice of older people this month. You may feel more current and in the loop, but you stand to gain plenty from their greater wisdom. Tigers prepared to learn will benefit a lot from taking this attitude. The learning curve is steep for those of you who are willing students. Use this month to push yourself beyond your limits. Success comes easily and without fuss, as long as you leave the door open and stop resisting efforts from others to help you. Shake off that Tiger pride; the more humble you are, the more you will gain.

WORK & CAREER - *Good Opportunities*

There are people in powerful places helping you, whether directly or behind the scenes. Being on the good side of your boss is vital to your success this month. Work closely with your superiors. Don't let them forget you exist, because out of sight is out of mind when it comes to promotion time.

While you have good support from your superiors, your subordinates may give you some problems this month. Don't let those who work for you get away with insubordination or it may become a habit. If you are offered the chance to take on more responsibilities, do so. This month you can triumph over your rivals and really stand out from the rest, so it is worth putting in the extra effort.

BUSINESS – *Door Open for You*

Many doors open for those of you in business, especially if you know the right people. Step up your efforts at networking because you never know who you will meet. Put in the effort to cultivate friendships. The time could come soon when you need to call on the help of an acquaintance. Don't think too hard about whether or not to call; pick up the phone and set up a meeting. It could lead to a fabulous opportunity. This is a good time to expand your business or to diversify. Go after the big contracts. Luck is on your side and if you don't make the most of this auspicious time, it would be wasted.

LOVE & RELATIONSHIPS - *Magical*

Your love life is simply magical this month. You have many techniques up your sleeve and this is the month to use them. If you already have your eye on someone, they won't be able to resist your charms once you turn them on. This is a time when you have the upper hand in relationships. Don't allow yourself to be so desperate to fall in love that you compromise on your standards. Married Tigers enjoy their spouses more than ever, especially if you put in the effort. Your luck is superior if you're a couple than for single Tigers, so make the most of your married status!

EDUCATION - *Intellectually Stimulating*

Studying new concepts comes easily to the Tiger student this month. Your ability to understand complex ideas is fueled by the combination of stars in your chart. This month favors learning new things and your desire to grow intellectually is heightened. Broaden your horizons by venturing out of your textbooks and set syllabuses. This will hone your understanding and appreciation of your studies, and you could come to enjoy schoolwork a lot more than chilling out and lazing about!

7TH MONTH
Aug 8th - Sept 7th 2011

A MONTH TO BE ALERT & CAREFUL

Your run of good luck takes a breather, and obstacles may start to get in your way. However, this is probably a good reality check for you. You've been riding on cloud nine so long you may have started to take the good life a little too much for granted. Your problems will be short-lived, so don't let anything get you overly depressed. Take things a little carefully this month. Lie low, avoid scheduling important events and meetings for now. Look on this as an opportunity to take a break from the fast-paced existence some of you may have been living over the past few months.

WORK & CAREER - *Watch Your Step*

This is not an auspicious month for you, thus it is vitally important that you watch your step. A wrong move may cost you dearly. Keep your emotions in check and don't let things get personal at the workplace. Keep your professional and personal lives separate. Mixing them is never such a great idea, and especially this month, when things could go very wrong if you're not careful. Office politics may rear its ugly head. Avoid becoming a victim of this by protecting yourself with a **Rooster** on your work desk or a jade cicada. Don't engage in petty gossip yourself. Watch your words carefully as some blabbermouth could repeat them after massaging the truth, causing some harm. Not a good time to try anything too different or to change jobs. Maintain the status quo till your luck improves next month.

BUSINESS – *Avoid Acting on Rumors*

You get hard hit by the misfortune star this month, so refrain from taking risks in business. You'll have to run a tighter ship and may have to keep expenses in check. Watch your cashflow and don't let yourself get into a cash bind. Avoid important discussions and meetings this month. Business ventures started now are likely to be flawed, with little chance of success, so it is better to save grand plans for implementation later.

Emergency issues may arise which stress you out, but which you can deal with as long as you keep your head. Avoid acting on rumors. There may be troublemakers about the place, causing a rift between you and key partners or business associates. Always make sure you have the whole story before you take any action. Ignorance may be you weak link this month, but as long as you know this, you know what to do about it.

LOVE & RELATIONSHIPS - *Misunderstandings*

Misunderstandings with your partner could leave you feeling sorry for yourself. When you disagree over an issue, reflect at the problems at hand before insisting your partner is in the wrong. Try to look at everything objectively. Avoid taking things personally. It is better to give in if there's an issue you can't resolve. Learn to laugh things off and you won't feel so bad when your partner inadvertently says something offensive. For the single Tigers, avoid striking up a new relationship this month. Love luck returns next month, so hold off for the next four weeks if you are looking for something that will last.

EDUCATION - *Get Organized*

Things could be a little frustrating this month. Careless mistakes, misplaced assignments, missed deadlines are all possibilities. Don't let yourself get stressed or hassled by it. Learn to schedule and organize yourself better. Don't let your social life get in the way of your school work, especially if this is an important time for you. Those of you on school holiday, relax and should rest your mind. Don't touch the books till term restarts because a clear mind will give you a fabulous advantage when school begins again next term.

8TH MONTH
Sept 8th - Oct 7th 2011

ROMANCE COULD
CAUSE SOME DISTRACTION

This is a highly passionate month for the Tiger when you could find your heart ruling your head. For some of you, this could present the opportunity of your life. Enjoyment is certainly there for the taking for those with little responsibility of home and family. But married Tigers should beware of the threat of external romance. Outside temptations are great and sometimes costly. Don't be fooled by what first seems innocent flirting; things can get out of hand very quickly if you don't stay alert to its possibilities.

Even for those single among you, don't let what disguises itself as romance cloud your judgment when it comes to work and your career. The number 4 star can play havoc with your life if you let it. Keep it under control and let it work for you. It brings scandal but also creativity and scholastic aptitude. Be sure to activate the positive aspect of this star.

WORK & CAREER – *Beware Office Romances*

How the month turns out very much depends on your situation. You may face a lack of mental concentration with your thoughts drifting off elsewhere. This makes it a bad time for deciding on important issues. Because your feelings are intensified this month, it is not the time to make big changes when it comes to your work. Do not change jobs this month. You are prone to acting rashly and you don't want to make a bad decision in haste.

Avoid office romances. There is a propensity towards this, but if you allow it to happen, it probably won't end well. The best way to make the most of this month is to direct your passion into producing really excellent work. This will get you noticed by your superiors, bringing you closer to that promotion you're after. It will also keep you out of trouble.

BUSINESS – *Think out of the Box*

Make the most of your creative flair this month. Do not be afraid to innovate. Look at new ways to do things, and new things to do. Competition may be fierce, but instead of trying to beat the competition, look at ways to make the competition irrelevant. Think out of the box. The original thinkers among you will get ahead this month. Be as eccentric as you want;

this could help you break away from old habits that have become stale. Focus on marketing strategy. If you already have a good product to sell, look at better ways of selling it. Business and wealth luck is good, you just need to try harder if you want to tap it.

LOVE & RELATIONSHIPS - *Beware Scandal*
This is a passionate month when your libido threatens to play havoc with your life. Married Tigers ought to be especially careful, because infidelity issues can become a problem. One false move is enough to cause a huge mess. Spend more time with your partner and channel your romantic feelings in this direction instead. Beware of flattering advances from charming troublemakers; a moment's folly could do irreparable damage to your marriage. Single Tigers have it better with more than one person vying for your attention. But scandal is possible nevertheless, so don't let yourself be too easy.

EDUCATION - *Great Study Luck*
Student Tigers have a great month ahead when study luck peaks. Make full use of this time to really listen and learn from others. Those of you taking exams are likely to do very well as long as you put in the work beforehand.

9TH MONTH
Oct 8th - Nov 6th 2011

QUARRELSOME VIBES SPOIL YOUR GOOD FEELING

The next four weeks are characterized by conflicting opinions, opposing views and inner demons. All this makes you particularly irritable and more easily riled by others. You may find it difficult to decide things for yourself this month, but at the same time you're unlikely to take kindly to others holding a divergent view from your own. Don't allow yourself to get stuck in a rut being indecisive. Leave the really big decisions till another time. For the small things, tell yourself it doesn't matter what you decide one way or another. But if you ask others for their opinion, learn to listen.

WORK & CAREER - *Stop Being Disagreeable*

Your quarrelsome mood follows you to the workplace and threatens to see you arguing frequently with your colleagues. Stop yourself when you find you are disagreeing just to be difficult. Sometimes you may argue not because you really believe in your cause, but because you are doing it out of habit. Stop this habit because it can get terribly annoying for others.

You could also find yourself rather distracted, which may slow your productivity at work. If you are in a competitive environment at work, others may overtake you. Keep your mind on the job and your temper in check. Carry the **Ping peace amulet** to improve your disposition; this will make things a lot easier for you when it comes to getting the job done and making a good impression on the boss.

BUSINESS – *Economize*

Money matters are in a down cycle this month, so economize where you can. Do not make big purchases or investments. Because you are prone to loss this month, you need to protect your financials. Sleep with a Lock Coin under your pillow to safeguard your wealth. Make sure you are insured; you could face a lawsuit from an unsatisfied customer. There will be many challenges to face, preventing you from taking a much-needed holiday right now. A weekend of unwinding will be good for you, but keep your mobile phone switched on; urgent matters may need your attention.

Carry the **Ping peace amulet** to help dissolve quarrelsome vibes this month.

LOVE & RELATIONSHIPS - *Loosen Up*

You may be taking yourself way too seriously right now. Loosen up and take things with a pinch of salt. Stop lusting over conquests you cannot have and the person who really is right for you will then have a chance to come forward. You may be scaring people off with your attitude. Take a step back and watch you're not coming across too desperate or too needy. Not a great time to jump into a new relationship. Married Tigers should watch you don't fly off the handle at your spouse for the smallest thing. The more argumentative you are, the more you will cause your partner to respond in exactly the same way.

EDUCATION - *Perfectionist*

A difficult month for the young Tiger. Your subjects may be difficult and you could find yourself loaded with more work than you can handle. Look to the long-term when making plans. Don't worry too much if you have to rush an assignment and hand in something you know you could have done better. You are saddled with the perfectionist syndrome right now, and the more picky you are, the more frustrated you'll get. Accept that things cannot always be perfect and you'll not only enjoy yourself more, you'll do better too!

10TH MONTH
Nov 7th - Dec 6th 2011

REDUCING ENERGY CAUSES ILLNESS

You suffer from reducing energy and also the appearance of the illness star this month. This puts you at greater risk of falling sick and catching viruses. You may be overcome with feelings of lethargy every now and again. Get over it by inspiring yourself to do something useful this month. You may be feeling the monotony of daily living. If you feel stuck in a rut, pull yourself out of it by taking up a new hobby. A new interest could inject much-needed spark into your life right now. Love luck is better than your luck in general, so this could be a good time to turn your attention to matters of the heart.

WORK & CAREER – *Avoid Daydreaming*

You could find it more difficult to get tasks completed well and on time in a month when your energy levels are flagging. Spend more time planning how you will approach each task before you start or you could end up having to do double work. Wear a **twelve-eye Dzi** to keep your energy levels up. Avoid daydreaming in the office or it will only accentuate your problem.

It is easy to fall behind your co-workers in a period like this. Work with your colleagues, not against them, because trying to do everything alone will only highlight your flaws this month. With allies you can get by without anyone noticing you're not quite putting in your 100%. Things improve tremendously next month, so for now, hang in there.

BUSINESS - *Think Things Through*

Obstacles arise, which although small, will affect your frame of mind and ability to think straight. Your difficulty in focusing and making sound decisions suggests this is a good time to go on holiday and let your business run itself for a while. If you're usually very hands on and do-it-yourself kind of boss, you'll certainly welcome some help this month. You may consider hiring some part-timers, particularly if you're in an industry where business speeds up at year-end. When things happen that surprise you, be sure to think things through before responding if you want to make the best decisions possible.

LOVE & RELATIONSHIPS - *Comfortable*

Tigers already in relationships will find they have a comfortable rapport with their partners, and this month is more about gentle loving and caring, rather than wild passion and bedroom activity. You'll enjoy being pampered and looked after. If your partner is the sort to always give in to you, you'll feel right at home this month. But if not, you may start feeling sorry for yourself. Although you may not be at your 100%, don't cry wolf too many times or you'll eventually be ignored. No one puts up with a hypochondriac for long. If you want to be mollycoddled, you'll have to do as much giving as taking.

EDUCATION - *Avoid Dangerous Sports*

You're likely to do well in subjects that interest you, and you are full of self initiative. Those who will go far in their academic career are those of you who are pro-active about your work. Do more than you have to, and don't look on completing assignments as a chore. Your horoscope chart indicates danger of sporting accidents, so don't take chances if you're involved in physical sports. Keep yourself healthy by keeping fit, but don't play rough this month. Avoid high risk sports altogether if you cannot do it safely.

The **12 eyed Dzi** will benefit the Tiger person this month, countering the low energy indication in your chart.

11TH MONTH
Dec 7th - Jan 5th 2012

BACK ON TOP AND GETTING STRONGER

This month things pick up for you again and your luck takes an upward turn. The double white stars in your chart bring you victory luck and the ability to triumph over the competition. Tiger people involved in any competitive situation will find it easy to beat the competition. Your mood is also better as your energy levels are up. Enjoy the month because not only is wealth and business luck good, personal happiness also comes more easily. There may be some changes in your life this month, as a transformational time is upon you, but any change will be for the better.

WORK & CAREER - *Promotion Luck*

You'll be kept extremely busy this month, with plenty of projects to see through, as well as new ones to start up. You may start to feel the pressure building up, especially if there are many deadlines to meet, but don't allow yourself to get stressed out. That will only make you less productive, which will cause you more stress. It is a vicious cycle, so don't fall into this trap. This month rest assured that your luck is very good, and your flexibility to change will be your secret weapon. This is a worthwhile time to go all out for that promotion you've been eyeing. Stay diligent in the workplace and don't give anyone reason to criticize you. Activate promotion luck with a **Monkey sitting on a Horse**.

BUSINESS – *Good Month for New Initiatives*

Business luck is good this month. New products and services introduced will do well. Launches and openings are excellent if they are held this month. Anything started this month will have a good chance of success. Without really trying, things will tend to fall into place for you. Carry the **Victory Banner** or place one on your desk to activate the superb combination of stars that have flown into your sector.

This is an ideal time to get going on new initiatives. Always plan for important business decisions to be taken during months that are auspicious for you, and this month everything goes well! While you should continue to run your ship with a sensible degree of caution, you can take more risks without danger of being badly burnt. Your aptitude to lead is enhanced by the presence of the lucky stars in your chart, so use this time to motivate your staff and business partners.

LOVE & RELATIONSHIPS – *Riding High*

Your love luck is riding high and this is where you will outshine all your contemporaries. If you're looking for something long term, there is every opportunity for you to find the right partner this month. Do not settle for second best. If you have recently come out of a relationship, do not enter straightaway into a rebound one. If you are patient, the person destined to be your soul mate will turn up. You can help things along by going out, meeting people and being generally sociable. The more you put yourself out there, the more chance you have of being swept off your feet and into a whirlwind romance.

EDUCATION – *Appetite for Knowledge*

Young Tigers in school will find themselves more motivated than usual this month. Your schoolwork will excite you in a way that may feel alien to you. Use this to your advantage by acting on your newfound drive. There is some danger that you may find your subjects at school so easy it borders on monotony. Be disciplined about finishing the work that you are set, but feel free to explore beyond your syllabus if it takes your fancy. There are so many ways for you to grow at this age; use your appetite for knowledge wisely.

12TH MONTH
Jan 6th - Feb 3rd 2012

AUSPICIOUS NEW YEAR AWAITS

2012 begins with much promise, as the Rabbit year comes to an end and the Dragon year waits to begin. There is plenty of Fire energy in your chart this much, which combines with a Water star to create power and completion energy. This brings you good business and wealth luck, so those of you helming an organization will do very well indeed this month. You are met with many exciting new opportunities, some of them too good to miss. Choosing between them and dividing your time and resources well will be your dilemma this month. Work aside, your personal life is also very promising this month. The Tiger looking for love will find it looking back. There's plenty of passion in your life, and you can crank it up as much as you're comfortable with.

WORK & CAREER - *Things Get Busy*

Things get busy at the workplace. You don't mind when it's your own work, but when it comes to doing other people's work for them, it may start to grate on your nerves. You may have to back up a colleague and even cover up for him or her on more than one occasion this month. Lending a helping hand is not a bad thing, considering you'll probably need a similar favor sometime in the future. Go with the flow. You're busy but you'll cope. And your luck is so good that something wonderful is bound to come out of it.

BUSINESS - *Exciting Opportunities*

Business luck looks brighter than ever. Your success this month will be built on good relationships so use your goodwill to further your causes. News you hear from third parties comes in especially useful, so keep your ears wide open. There are some exciting opportunities that open up for you. Do not shrug off extreme ideas. Consider everything that comes your way. This is also a good time to improve internal operations. Pay attention to details. Little tweaks here and there can make a big difference this month. When it comes to decision making, go with your instincts, as your judgment is good this period. Don't let yourself be swayed by an outsider whose intentions though well-meaning may not coincide directly with your own.

LOVE & RELATIONSHIPS - *Passionate*

Fabulous love luck for the Tiger-born this month!
Passion runs high, affecting all your romantic
relationships. Be careful there's not more than one.
You could find yourself being pulled in different
directions, with more than one person vying for your
attention. Be charming to everyone, but watch you
don't give your heart so easily, or it could be just as
easily broken. Enjoy yourself this month but don't play
with fire. Married Tigers could be feeling distinctly
playful, and if your partner does not play ball, you
could find yourself looking elsewhere to entertain
yourself. As long as you keep the fun clean and decent,
you can enjoy the month with no dire consequences.
But avoid starting anything outside of your marriage
if you value what you have with your spouse.

EDUCATION - *Good Potential*

Be considerate of the feelings of the people you care
about. You may disagree over certain things, but if
your parents or those looking after you advise you in
a certain way, listen to them and be prepared to take
good advice. Young Tigers may be a little wayward
this month, but if kept in check, can channel their
energy to doing really well in their studies.

Important Feng Shui Updates for 2011

Part 6

If you have been following the advice given in these Fortune & Feng Shui books on annual feng shui updates, you are already familiar with the time dimension of feng shui which protects against negative luck each year.

This requires overall cleansing and re-energizing of the energy of the home to prepare for the coming of a new year, while simultaneously making placement changes to accommodate a new pattern of chi distribution. Getting rid of old items and replacing with specially made new remedial cures that are in tune with the year's chi brings pristine and fresh new luck into the home.

It is truly vital to anticipate and quickly suppress the source of malicious chi brought by the year's new feng shui winds as this ensures that bad chi born in afflicted sectors never have a chance to gather, accumulate, grow strong and then ripen in a burst of bad luck! With powerful remedies in place, this will not happen, thereby keeping residents safe from the kind of harm that can be unsettling and heartbreaking.

Severe bad luck can happen to anyone; sometimes, even in the midst of some personal triumphant moment, your world can suddenly crumble. Last year for instance, the world witnessed the incredibly sad falling apart of the marriages of **Kate Winslet** and **Sandra Bullock** soon after they each had reached the pinnacle of their profession by winning the Oscar for Best Actress.

Kate had won in 2009 and Sandra in 2010. Both had breathlessly thanked their husbands obviously unaware of destructive energies lurking within their homes. Both husbands - for whatever reasons - were looking for gratification outside their marriages! Kate's husband, noted Director Sam Mendes' eyes had already started roving in 2009... but the marriage fell apart in 2010 when the star of infidelity made its appearance.

Both actresses do not believe in luck… it is safe to assume they are too busy to arrange for the placement of feng shui cures in their homes.

Those not following time dimension feng shui from these books are unlikely to have known that last year 2010 was a year when the *external romance star of peach blossom* was lurking in every household, creating the potential to cause havoc in marriages! It was vital last year to place cures in the home to protect against outsider third party interference. Sandra Bullock and Kate Winslet are just two of the high profile victims of the star of *External Peach Blossom*! They are exquisitely beautiful ladies, but both of their marriages unraveled in March of 2010!

It is therefore so important that each time we cross into a new year, we should note the particular ailments and afflictions of the year, and then carefully bring in the antidotes so we can sail through the year without having to endure the consequences of bad feng shui, which of course can manifest in different ways. No matter how it manifests, bad luck always brings distress, heartbreak and a sense of helplessness.

Why go through this kind of unhappiness when you can prevent or reduce it?

Each year there will be the same kinds of afflictions bringing illness, accidents, robbery, quarrels and severe misfortune, but these afflictions change location each year and vary in strength from year to year. So we need to systematically suppress these *"staples of bad luck"* first.

Then there are the disturbing stars of misfortune - these too need to be neutralized mainly with element therapy so that they do not cast their ill influence onto your luck. In some years, there can be some hazardous or dangerous alignment of energies we need to be careful of, and these also need to be addressed. For instance, we have already told you about the four pillars of clashing elements bringing severe quarrelsome energy that can get violent.

It is SO vital, for Tiger-born to be alert to dangers in the bigger picture. This is a year when you need to make a concerted effort to protect yourself as you are indirectly afflicted by the side five yellow coming to you from the East. Do place the **five element pagoda with the tree of life** on your East to safeguard your house energy and everyone in it from getting hit by the five yellow affliction.

Incense are a powerful way of transcending time and space, blending heaven and earth energies to chase away all the afflictions that bring disaster, setbacks and accidents. In fact, incense and scents, although invisible, are such a powerful way of overcoming obstacles that they have been used by all the major traditions of the world.

The use of incense is one of the most powerful ways of overcoming all kinds of obstacles that may be blocking your luck. The use of incense is part of spiritual feng shui - the third dimension of inner feng shui that can make such a difference to really allowing great good fortune into your life.

The use of incense is one of the most powerful way to overcome obstacles and create good fortune.

This is because creating a regular infusion of incense (with some smoke) works incredibly well for clearing the pathway for good chi energy to flow into your home; and with empowering symbolic placements, these work together to create the lucky ambience you need. Home energy then becomes harmonious and benevolent, blending beautifully with new patterns of chi formations that are flowing through your home. Just try infusing your space with the special blend of sandalwood or pine incense and feel the difference instantly! Focusing on your house feng shui from this perspective will help you enjoy a better year irrespective of how good or how bad the indications for the year may be. This is because the correct kind of aromas can go a long way to subduing the afflictions in all the afflicted corners of the house, hence protecting everyone in the household.

Misfortunes are always worse and have nastier consequences when they creep up on you. These come in many ways, for instance, when confronted with the prospect of losing your job, your home, your good name, your child, your lover or your spouse.

It is only when afflictive energies are suppressed that bad happenings become manageable. They can even be avoided. This is the wonderful promise and benefit of creating good and timely feng shui in the home.

And when divine assistance is invoked through the wearing of powerful amulets and sacred talismans, the remedies become even more effective. This brings harmony and smooth sailing through the year.

Luck is Never Static

Luck always occur in cycles and the key to continuing good fortune is to know when the luck of your house is at its peak and when it requires extra protection. When important parts of the house you live in get hit by misfortune-bringing stars, everyone living within gets hurt. In the same way, when these same areas are visited by lucky stars, everyone in the house enjoys good fortune. To what degree this incidence of good and bad luck affects residents depends also on their personal outlook for the year. Cycles of luck affect different people in different ways and this is one reason why it is so beneficial to analyze how the year affects your animal sign.

Consider the infinite variations of each individual's pattern of luck when you factor in the two sets of elements in the four sets of birth data - Year, Month, Day and Hour of Birth... then factor in the house, the locations of the main door, the bedroom, the dining and living area. Factor in also the changing energies of the year, as well as the energy of the people who surround you, who make up your circle of family and friends... and you will be awed by the mathematical combinations of chi that are affecting you every single moment!

We cannot take care of everything that affects our luck, but we sure can take care of enough to ensure a pretty good and smooth year.

Once we are assured that we have been adequately protected against sudden misfortunes, we can then turn our attention to maximizing and magnifying good fortune for the year... Success, Love, Satisfaction with Life, Money, Wealth, Career highs, Contentment... and a lot more can then be induced to manifest into our lives.

This depends on what we want, what we energize for and how we enhance our bedrooms, work spaces and living areas.

It is really easier than you think! Just protect against bad luck and energize for good luck.

You must first protect your **main door** and your **bedroom**. The location of these two important parts of your house must be protected against bad numbers or bad stars. Afflictive energy can be illness or misfortune numbers, hostile or robbery stars. These can, together with other kinds of negative energy, cause loss of some kind. Someone might force you into litigation - this is something that will happen more than normal this year; you might suffer perhaps a break up of an important relationship - this too is unfortunately being fanned by the destructive patterns of elements this year.

Severe bad luck or loss, when it manifests, is always traumatic. Feng shui corrections offer the solutions to avoiding or at least diminishing negativities happening. Knowing feng shui enables you to anticipate a potentially problematic year; and then to do something about it.

Correcting and suppressing bad energy is rarely difficult. But it requires a bit of effort. What you must do is systematically go through each of the nine sectors of your home, mentally dividing each level of your home into a three by three sector grid that corresponds to eight compass directions with a center.

The next step is to study the year's charts; first, the Annual Feng Shui chart which pinpoints the afflicted parts of the home, then the 24 mountain charts which show the "*stars*", both lucky and unlucky, that also influence the year's distribution of luck, and finally, the year's four pillars chart. It is the collective and unified analysis of these indications that point to what needs to be done to safeguard the feng shui of any abode.

Suppressing
Flying Star Afflictions for the Year

SE	SOUTH	SW
6	2	4
5 (FIVE YELLOW) / EAST	7	9 / WEST
1	3	8
NE	NORTH	NW

Traditionally, one of the more important things to update prior to each new year is to find the new locations for all the afflictive star numbers and then to deal with each of them. These yearly afflictions are the same each year, but their strength and severity vary from year to year, depending on where they are. The element of each affliction interacts with the element of the sector they fly into. In some years for instance, the misfortune star number of five yellow a.k.a. **wu wang** can be really strong, while in some years it is weaker.

In 2011, for instance, the *wu wang* flies to the East, where its Earth element is strongly suppressed by the Wood element here. The 2011 *wu wang* is thus not as strong as it was in the previous year when it occupied the Southwest. There, the Earth element of the SW strengthened the *wu wang*.

In 2011 therefore we are not so afraid of this otherwise feared star. In spite of this, it is still advisable to keep the *wu wang* under control in case someone in the house is going through weak Life Force or whose Spirit Essence may be lacking. The Ox's personal chi essence is quite low, so the *wu wang* can well be a threat.

Remedies against the Wu Wang

So do place the traditional remedies to suppress *wu wang* in the East anyway, because this is a thoroughly unpleasant star whose effect could suddenly manifest if your bedroom happens to be affected by it and is also being hit by some secret unknown poison arrow, which can act as a catalyst for the *wu wang* to erupt; or when the Wood element here gets inadvertently weakened for whatever reason.

The *wu wang* blocks success and it affects the luck of the eldest son of the family. So to be safe, get the cures that have been specially designed for the year and place these in the East sectors. Do not forget the East walls of your important rooms and also the living and family areas where you and your family spend a great deal of time. Place the cures on a sideboard or table, not on the floor!

Five Element Pagoda with Tree of Life

In 2011 we are recommending the five element pagoda that comes with a wood base and is decorated with an all-powerful Tree of Life that grows from the base of the pagoda right to the tip. There are three pairs of birds on the branches of the tree of life. These birds bring opportunities from the cosmic constellations and legend has it they attract exactly the kind of luck a household needs. From the leaves of the tree hang glittering jewels which signify the treasures of the earth, the element that symbolizes wealth and prosperity in 2011.

This powerful five element pagoda is actually a transforming tool which turns the all powerful wu wang into a wealth enhancing tool. It greatly benefits everyone whose Kua number is 5 and for the Tiger-born, this will be the Lady Metal Tiger (61 years old) and the Lady Fire Tiger (25 years old). Both of you will benefit enormously from this symbol of protection. Note that this particular pagoda with

the tree of life synchronizes extremely well with the
energies of 2011 and 2012 when the wu wang flies to
the wood sectors of the compass. It is usually not used
during other years.

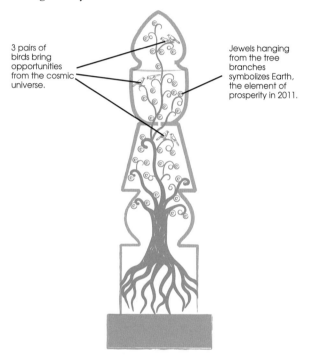

3 pairs of
birds bring
opportunities
from the cosmic
universe.

Jewels hanging
from the tree
branches
symbolizes Earth,
the element of
prosperity in 2011.

The five element pagoda with Tree of Life
transforms the wu wang into a wealth-bringing star.

Metal Bell with Tree of Life

Another very beneficial cure for the 2011 wu wang is the powerful Bell which is also made of metal but has a wooden mallet so the sound created is mellower and lower than that of an all-metal bell. The handle of the bell is made of wood; and on the bell itself there is again the amazing tree of life to strengthen the wood chi of the East; and the tree also has 6 birds on its branches; and with jewels on its leaves to signify wealth luck.

This transforms the five element bell into an empowering, enhancing tool which, even as it suppresses the wu wang, is simultaneously sending out powerful vibrations each time the sounds of the bell are created. This way the bell utilizes the wu wang to attract great good fortune opportunities and it is by placing a tree of life with 6 birds that gives it these attributes. We have also embossed the *dependent arising mantra* onto both the five element bell and pagoda. This powerful mantra greatly empowers these cures! Those wanting to wear these powerful

The **Metal Bell** with wooden handle is another enhancing tool that simultaneously suppresses the wu wang.

symbols over the two years 2011 and 2012 can consider wearing either the pagoda or the bell with the tree design to safeguard themselves from the *wu wang*.

The Tiger-born must be extra careful in June as this is the month when the Five Yellow can be dangerous. But placing the *wu wang* cures here would benefit you very much and this is because the *wu wang* is very strong in your home location of Northeast.

Misfortunes caused by the wu wang in 2011 are not as severe as in other years, but they are nonetheless annoying and aggravating. It can cause problems with employees or act as a catalyst for other kinds of bad luck to erupt, so it is a good idea to suppress its negative effect. This year's cure does just that but it also uses the inherent strength of the *wu wang* to transform bad luck into something good.

If you reside in a room located in the East sector of your house, place the pagoda inside your bedroom. Make sure it is in place before February 3rd which is the start of the Lunar New Year 2011. It is also important to take note that there should not be any renovations done in the East side of the house through

2011. Avoid all kinds of demolition or digging work although there are some feng shui masters who say that building works are not harmful, arguing that anything productive will not harm the household. We disagree with this as the *wu wang* should not be activated by any kind of building. This only strengthens it. Planting a tree in the East is however auspicious, especially if you do this on February 4th the day of the *lap chun*!

Planting a tree on the 4th February, the day of the Lap Chun, is extremely auspicious!

Other Afflictions of the 2011 Chart

SE	SOUTH	SW
6	2 ILLNESS STAR	4
EAST 5	7	9 WEST
1	3	8
NE	NORTH	NW

The Illness Star flies to the South in 2011

This is an Earth element star flying into a Fire sector, so here, the illness star gets considerably strengthened, making it a serious threat to residents, but especially for anyone residing in the South sector of the house; but the illness star affects everyone if it is where the main door into the house is located. Any house that faces or sits South will find that residents within are more vulnerable to catching viruses and falling ill more easily.

Should the main door of the house be in the South, the constant opening and closing of the door will energize the star making it more likely to bring illness into the house and this is pronounced during the months of March and December when the month stars mirror that of the year hence bringing a double whammy to afflicted sectors.

If your door is facing South, it is a good idea to use another door located in another sector (if possible) especially during these two months. If this is not possible then it is necessary to exhaust the Earth element of the illness star placing something metallic or made of wood here. It is necessary also to remove all earth element items such as crystals, porcelain vases or stone objects. Also keep lights in the South dim to reduce Fire element energy.

Cures for the Illness Star of 2011

Over the years we have found the best way to suppress illness energy brought by the intangible flying star 2 is with a **wu lou** shaped container made of metal - either in brass or steel. The wu lou is a container for keeping herbal cures so that over the years it has come to signify medicinal qualities. Many popular deities such as the **Goddess of**

Mercy, Kuan Yin, carry a small wu lou shaped little bottle that contains healing nectar. Placing a large wu lou in the South generates invisible healing energies for both physical and mental afflictions. It is an excellent idea to place a small wu lou by your bedside so that it exudes healing energies as you sleep. This is good feng shui!

You can also invoke the help of the powerful healing Buddha, also known as the **Medicine Buddha**. This is the blue Buddha who create enormous blessings in any home that displays his image or mantra in any way at all, especially in the sector where the flying illness star is located. The Medicine Buddha ensures that all residents enjoy good health, rarely if ever falling sick. It is a good idea in 2011 to have an image of the Medicine Buddha placed on a table top in the North part of any room where you spend time.

Those feeling poorly in 2011 should also wear **Medicine Buddha bracelets** or our specially designed

moving mantra watches - the only watches of its kind in the world! We brought out the first such moving mantra watch last year and they have since helped so many people that we have extended our range to include a watch with the healing image of the Medicine Buddha.

Wearing such a watch is like having prayers being constantly recited for your good health. It is truly amazing how far technology has progressed. To us, it makes sense to utilize all the technical advances that have made so many wonderful new products possible. Many of the advances in technology have made feng shui very easy to practice.

Wear the **watch** with the healing image of **Medicine Buddha** if you are feeling poorly.

The Quarrelsome Hostile Star flies to the North in 2011

This is a Wood element star flying into a Water element sector. As such this noisy, litigation bringing star number is both strong and harder to overcome. It is dangerous and aggravating and very capable of causing anyone staying in the North sector a great deal of problems.

This is the major affliction affecting the North sector in 2011. There is stress which could well affect your productivity and for some of you can even be the cause of delay and obstacles. At its worst, the effect of this affliction is someone taking you to court, causing you aggravations and inconvenience. Someone whose room is here might also get violent.

This star brings a pervasive feeling of hostility, short tolerance levels and a great deal of impatience. There will be arguments, fights and misunderstandings for everyone directly hit by it.

Unfortunately for anyone having a bedroom in the North sector of the house, the quarrelsome star 3 is made stronger this year because its Wood Element is produced even more by the Water element of the North. As a Wood element star, the best way to subdue its effect is to exhaust it with Fire Element energy. Anything that suggests Fire is an excellent cure, so bright lights and the color red are excellent remedies. Hence, because the North is associated with Water energy, the danger is enhanced, so remedying it is vital.

An excellent cure against the 3 star is the **Red Dragon amulet**. This brings luck while keeping the number 3 star subdued. It is excellent for anyone having their bedroom in the North or those living in homes with main doors that face North. Note that this amulet has the Dragon carrying a sword in its right claw as this helps overcome all the clashing elements of the year.

The Violent Star 7 attracts bad people into the home

SE	SOUTH	SW
6	2	4
5	7 VIOLENT STAR	9
1	3	8
NE	NORTH	NW

The Violent star 7 is in the center of the chart this year, where it is symbolically locked up, hence reducing its influence. This is an affliction which hurts most when it occupies one of the outer sectors of any building, but trapped in the center, its negative impact is less severe.

The number 7 star number is an Metal element number and with the center being an Earth sector, here we have a situation of Earth producing Metal, so while it may be hemmed in in the center, it is nevertheless troublesome. It is a number that causes loss through being cheated or robbed.

A good way of keeping this affliction under wraps is simply to place a small sideboard in the center of the house, place seven pieces of metal within and then lock it up. This symbolically "locks up" the number 7 star very effectively. At the same time, have a **Rhino with an Elephant** near the entrance into the home.

However, should any of you be feeling vulnerable with the burglary star in the center of the home, you can safeguard yourself by carrying the **blue-colored Rhino** or using it as a hanging on your bags or hung in the car. It is good practice to stay protected against encountering bad people who would want to harm you. Use the **Blue Rhino protector** as this continues to be an effective cure in 2011. It is a highly respected cure against the potential violence of the 7.

Note that the problem with the number 7 star in 2011 is that being in the center of the feng shui chart, the number 7 can potentially spread its influence into any part of the house, hence it is necessary to keep it well under control. The best is to literally "lock it up", otherwise it simply plays havoc with house security. It is very inconvenient and even dangerous when the 7 star number strikes.

Carry **a blue-colored Rhino hanging** to stay protected against encountering bad people and those who do not have your best interests at heart.

In 2011 the God of the Year cannot be ignored

The Tai Sui is important because this year, it directly faces the *star of natural disaster* in the West sector of the chart. This is a 24 mountain star that sits between the two stars of *three killings*! That there are such intensive negative stars directly confronting the Tai Sui is not good for the year. It suggests a battle, and when a battle takes place, there is always collateral damage!

Especially when they are read against the background of the year's clashing elements in the four pillars, these signs collectively indicate clear and present danger. How the dangers of the year manifest will vary in timing and severity for different houses and different countries; but generally, an afflicted Tai Sui means that the wars of the world currently being waged on several fronts are unlikely to decline. There is also no let up in the occurrence of natural disasters.

It is therefore important to be extra mindful of the Tai Sui in 2011. Avoid confronting it. Avoid facing East and make extra efforts not to "disturb" its location, the East sector of the house. This sector must be kept quiet as noise activates the Tai Sui and incurs its wrath. Also avoid digging, banging or renovating this side of the home.

It is beneficial to place a well-executed art piece of the beautiful Pi Yao in the East, as this celestial creature appeases the Tai Sui. The Pi Yao brings good feng shui. You can find many artistic variations of this auspicious creature all over China and Hong Kong. It is a great favorite with people who believe in feng shui as it brings exceptional good fortune into the home. For 2011, a Pi Yao made in Earth element material is preferred as this element signifies wealth luck. So crystal or ceramic Pi Yao, or one made in liu li, would be excellent.

It is important for everyone whose bedroom is in the East, or whose sitting direction while working is facing or sitting East, to place the Pi Yao near you; It does not matter if the Pi Yao is standing or sitting but it should appear proud and majestic looking. The more beautiful looking the Pi Yao is the better it is to display in the house to appease the Tai Sui. *This advice applies to anyone irrespective of their animal sign.*

The place of the Tai Sui is taken very seriously in feng shui. It is emphasized in the Treatise on Harmonizing Times and Distinguishing Directions compiled under the patronage of the Qianlong Emperor during his reign in the mid Eighteenth century and any Master practicing feng shui in China or Hong Kong always ensures the Tai Sui is respected and thus taken account of in their updating process. The Emperor Qiang Lung inspired Treatise states that the locations where the Tai Sui resides and where the Tai Sui has just vacated are **lucky** locations. So note that in 2011, the locations of East and NE1 are considered lucky benefiting from the lingering energy of the Tai Sui. Those having their rooms in these two locations will enjoy the patronage and protection of the Tai Sui in 2011.

The Treatise further explains that it is **unlucky** to reside in the location where the Tai Sui is progressing towards i.e. clockwise on the astrology compass. In 2011 this means the Southeast 1 location; it is unlucky to directly confront the Tai Sui's residence. It is unlucky to "face" the Tai Sui because this is deemed rude, so the advice for 2011 is to not to directly face East.

In 2011, never forget to avoid confronting the Tai Sui. **Do not face East this year even if this is your success direction under the Kua formula of personalized lucky directions.** Those who forget and inadvertently face the Tai Sui run the risk of offending the Tai Sui. This brings obstacles to your work life. Your road to achieving success gets constantly interrupted and for some, supporters can turn into adversaries.

In 2011 the West of every building is afflicted by the Three Killings

SE	SOUTH	SW
6	2	4
5 (EAST)	7	9 3 KILLINGS (WEST)
1	3	8
NE	NORTH	NW

This affliction brings three severe misfortunes associated with loss, grief and sadness. Its location each year is charted according to the animal sign that rules the year. Thus in 2011 it flies to the West because the Rabbit belongs to the Triangle of Affinity made up of the Rabbit, Sheep and Boar; with the Rabbit occupying a cardinal direction (East).

The Three Killings is thus in the West, the direction that is directly opposite the Rabbit. This feng shui aggravation affects only primary directions, so unlike other feng shui afflictions, the direct bad effects of the *three killings* are felt over a larger area of the house.

When you suffer a sudden reversal of fortune, it is usually due to being hit by the three killings. In 2011 the *three killings* resides in the West, where it poses some danger to the young daughters of the family. Anyone occupying the West would be vulnerable to being hit by the *three killings*.

For everyone whose bedroom and/or main doors face West or are located in the West sector of your home, please get the **celestial protectors** - the Chi lin, Fu Dog and Pi Yao - preferably made colorful and with a fierce expression. Place them together on a coffee table or sideboard; get them in brass and enamel.

Carry the **three celestials amulet** to be protected against the **Three Killings** this year.

For them to be effective, some texts refer also to the three different deities traditionally seated on their backs, but as a feng shui cure, they are as effective on their own or with the deities, although the secret is to make sure they have their different **implements** with them, as these enable them to symbolically overcome the afflictions.

Thus the **Sword** on the back of the **Pi Yao** protects against loss of wealth. The **Lasso** on the back of the **Chi Lin** to protects against loss of loved one. The **steel hook** on the back of the **Fu Dog** protects against loss of good name. The hook is a very powerful implement which also "hooks in wealth luck".

Do not use antique images as feng shui cures as these are usually surrounded by tired chi. It is important that feng shui remedies have fresh energy so there is strong vigor and vitality chi attached to them. Antique furniture decorated with celestials can be lovely to look at, but they rarely make powerful cures. They can however generate auspicious chi after they are cleansed of lingering yin vibes. Use a dry cloth with either sea salt or crystal salt to wipe off stale chi and they should be fine. Do this cleansing ritual at least once a year. The month before the lunar new year is a good time. The energy of the *three killings* can sometimes stick onto furniture, especially those with animals or human images painted onto them. It is a good idea to use raw salt as a way of wiping off lingering bad chi. Those of who may want to stay protected from the *three killings* and prevent them from overwhelming you when you are out and about this year can also hang the **three celestials amulet** on your hand bags and pocket books.

Those of you staying in the West sectors of the house, you could experience bad dreams and nightmares and if so, make sure you place the **three celestial guardians** on a cabinet along the West wall of the room. If you have a window in the bedroom, place the three celestials there even if it is not the West wall. The presence of the three guardians is a powerful cosmic force that protects.

Strengthening the Right & Subduing the Left of the Tiger's Luck

The Tiger benefits from the stars of the 24 mountains in 2011 as this circle of cosmic energy brings one lucky star of *Big Auspicious* that comes to the right of the Tiger's location of Northeast 3. Hence in Northeast 2 the star is bringing to the Tiger the strong possibility of something very auspicious coming to it during the year; with the most likely month for anything spectacular coming being May, when the monthly

THE 24 MOUNTAIN STARS AND FENG SHUI CHART OF 2011

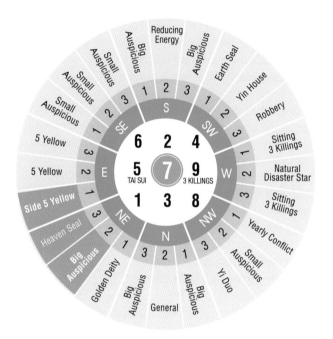

24 Mountains showing the Tiger direction being flanked by side 5 Yellow and Big Auspicious star.

star of 8 meets with the annual star of 1 to create the powerful double white combination of 8 and 1. This combination brings new growth energy for the Tiger. So keep your ears and eyes open.

To strengthen the 24 mountain star of Big Auspicious, you can enhance Northeast 2 with the physical presence of water. The year 2011 is a wonderful opportunity to tap into this lucky star by installing a small water feature in the Northeast 2 sector of the living area or of the house or garden. The water feature does not need to be big, but the presence of moving water here is beneficial for the year.

It is quite important to make certain you get the location just right, so stand in the center of the room which you want to activate the star of Big Auspicious. Then using a good 24 mountain type compass mark out the exact spot that corresponds to the Northeast 2. Here, place a **six tier waterfall** to activate water, and place this here for the duration of the year.

Activate money luck this year with a **water feature** in the Southeast.

On the Tiger's left however is the *wu wang* or five yellow, and in feng shui parlance, the Tiger is negatively affected by this *side five yellow*. This is considered an affliction and must be subdued with the **five element pagoda** with the **tree of life**. Place it in East 1 direction to keep this misfortune star from causing harm to you in 2011. Remember that placement feng shui works best when there is accuracy of compass readings so it is a good idea to invest in a good compass and to learn to take accurate compass readings.

Suppressing Anger Vibrations in the North

	SE	SOUTH	SW	
EAST	6	2	4	WEST
	5	7	9	
	1	3 (ANGRY STAR)	8	
	NE	NORTH	NW	

We have already noted that the North is the sector where the angry star 3 has flown to in 2011. This can be suppressed by using the **Red Dragon amulet**. Anger vibrations are what will cause problems for anyone residing in the North as this will block the manifestation of good fortune.

One of the best ways to prevent anger vibrations getting out of hand is to use two powerful rituals, both using the medium of incense. Scents, aromas, incense - these are powerful mediums that can transcend the cosmic fields of energy that affect us.

We have spent the past year talking about the third dimension of feng shui, and the use of aromatic incense is one of the more common ways used by Masters skilled in the shamanistic aspects of feng shui practice. At its most basic, joss sticks are used during the Wealth God welcoming rituals performed during the night before the lunar new year; during such rituals very pungent and strong smells such as sandalwood are used.

Incense can also be used through the year. They are a powerful medium that can be used to clear the air of negatives; to suppress troublesome energies that bring aggravations that disturb the mind of residents. Incense is usually associated with the transcendence of chi energy between cosmic realms of consciousness and are an advanced form of energy practices used in the old days by expert practitioners. They are powerful yet invisible instruments for dissolving concentrations of negative energy. The number 3 star is one example of a concentration of energy that brings aggravations. It is good feng shui to dissolve its effect.

An excellent way to stay immune to the 3 star therefore is to utilize calming aromas, and in the case of anyone staying in the North you can use incense for the outdoors and for your bedroom, you can try using lavender aroma which is relaxing and soothing when infused into the atmosphere.

What is more effective however is to perform the incense ritual which will get rid of anger vibrations very effectively. Incense also appease spiritual landlords in the area and they will help to suppress all negativities that cause hostile energy to burst into big quarrels.

Burn sandalwood or pine incense regularly in the North in 2011.

Activating the Trinity of Tien Ti Ren

In the year 2011 **all four primary directional locations** - North, South, East and West - are afflicted, as we have seen with the illness, hostile, five yellow and natural disaster star. of the four only the West location has the lucky 9 star number but 9 in a Metal element sector always contains hidden dangers; so correcting, and placing remedies to safeguard the cardinal locations of the house is extremely important in 2011.

The **four secondary directions** on the other hand, are indicating extremely lucky star numbers, with 8 leading the way as it flies into the patriarchal corner of Northwest, followed by the heavenly 6 in the opposite direction of Southeast. Then there is the victory star in the Northeast and the star of romance and scholarship in the Southwest in 2011.

With this kind of star number configurations, we also note that the Northeast/Southwest axis (which is the favorable axis of this current period of 8) has been blessed with the star of earth seal in the SW and the matching counterpart star of the heaven seal in the Northeast.

The presence of these heaven and earth stars are indicative of the need for the trinity of lucky cosmic forces to be present in the North and the South, the other set of axis direction which are showing a set of two *Big Auspicious* stars. In N1 and N3 and also in S1 and S3, we see here a quartet of important lucky stars brought by the circle of the 24 mountains.

In 2011, there is the strong indication of substantial changes taking place in the world which will bring benefits to some and loss to others. This is vital to understand, as the year itself is showing a set of four pillars which not only has 4 sets of clashing elements but also two yang and two yin pillars. This suggests that the complementarily of cosmic forces is balanced. Yin and yang are in balance.

Good fortune manifests as growth, sudden windfalls and big transformations of luck that bring a "*house filled with jewels*" enabling one to "*wear the jade belt*" if the household successfully activates the trinity of Tien Ti Ren. In other words, there must be plentiful supply of heaven, earth and mankind energies! This is something that is beneficial to ensure at all times but more so in 2011, where severe bad luck indications are balanced against equally powerful auspicious indications. So the important thing is to tap into the positive energies of the year, thereby getting on to the growth spiral. Tien ti ren is the key!

Symbolically, just placing the words heaven and earth are often good enough to complement the presence of people within a home. Mankind chi is the powerful yang chi that activates the yin earth chi and the cosmic heaven chi.

In the old days, wealthy households would always include miniature mountains to signify earth, and also all the deities of their faith - Taoism or Buddhism, the **8 Immortals** and the **18 holy beings** - all to signify heaven chi while at the same time imbuing their homes with activity and celebrations to signify mankind chi. This infusion of yang energy acts a catalyst to generate the presence of the powerful cosmic trinity.

In this way did wealthy households of the past live, and over the years, these practices came to signify the cultural underpinnings of the Chinese way of life. Thus one should not be surprised to note that many Chinese households believe that the blessing power of heaven is brought in by the presence of deities on their family altar. The family altar was always placed rather grandly, directly facing the front door.

This signified the continuing presence of heaven luck. It was important to keep the family altars clean with offerings of food, lights, water, wine and incense made daily. Wealthier households would even have professionals such as monks and holy men, who would come and recite prayers for the family at special dates in the year. These were daily rituals believed to keep the family patriarch safe and the household in a state of abundance. In other words, keeping their lifestyles secure.

In addition, good earth chi was assured by the presence of mountains and rivers simulated in landscaped gardens around the family home and symbolized by **mountain scenery paintings** inside the home. Good feng shui also ensures good chi flows in abundance through the rooms and corridors of the house.

Finally, excellent mankind chi is kept flowing fresh and revitalizing yang energy. Auspicious phrases and lucky rhyming couplets were placed as artistic calligraphy in important rooms of the house; this was the equivalent of today's very popular "*affirmations*".

The Chinese have been living with these powerful affirmations for as long as anyone can remember, and there are literally thousands of such lucky phrases such as "*your wealth has arrived*" or "*your luck is as long as the yellow river*"... and so forth.

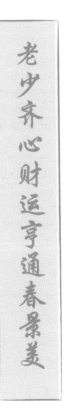

合家和睦致富路广鸿图展

老少齐心财运亨通春景美

The Chinese have been living with powerful affirmations for as long as anyone can remember. These affirmations often took the form of rhyming couplets, such as "*Your wealth is as long as the yellow river.*"

These are popular sayings exchanged between families during festive seasons and during Chinese New Year.

Anyone wanting to enjoy good fortune continuously must be mindful of the power generated by *tien ti ren* chi inside their homes. This is very timely for 2011 to help you benefit from the year. In 2011 therefore, the three dimensions of feng shui - space and time as well as the dimension which engages the cosmic force within the self (the purest source of yang energy generated from within you) must all be present. In fact, this is a major secret of feng shui. This is the mankind chi that pulls heaven and earth chi together.

Good mankind chi requires you to stay positive, to generate lucky aspirations and to anticipate good outcomes.

Your expectations must be high. You can enhance the empowerment of your own self. This unlocks for you the strength of mankind luck - *ren chi* - which pulls time and space into a powerful whole. With this kind of attitude, you can then start to enhance the four lucky secondary directions with powerful enhancing placement feng shui:

Enhancing the Chi of 8 in the Northwest

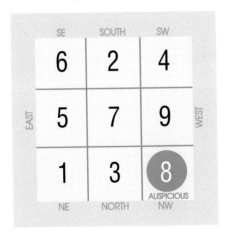

The all-powerful and auspicious 8 flies to the place of the patriarch in 2011, bringing quite exceptional great good fortune to all the father figures of the world.

Being located in the Northwest, the 8 Earth star also gets very considerably strengthened, and especially since it is flying to the NW from the center where it was located last year.

As an annual star number, the 8 is indeed very strong. It brings good relationship luck and it brings success and wealth. It is a powerful star at its zenith. What worked last year, the **crystal 8** embedded with real 24 carat gold, continues to work this year, so do display it in the Northwest of the house; or on your office.

But the crystal 8 becomes even more powerful when it is placed alongside a **crystal Ru Yi,** the scepter of authority. This is especially beneficial for Chief Executive Officers i.e. CEOs and bosses. In fact, anyone in a position of authority and power will benefit from the Ru Yi placed alongside the 8. In the old days, these symbols were recommended for mandarins at court - equivalent to the Ministers and top business leaders of today.

Place a Ru YI alongside a crystal 8 for career strength and longevity.

Those who want a boost to their career should definitely consider placing this powerful symbol of advancement and upward mobility in the Northwest corner of their home, of their office or their home office. With the 8 flying into the Northwest, the Ru Yi placed next to the 8 becomes especially effective. Place the Ruy in exactly the middle of the NW sector i.e. in NW2, as this is the auspicious part of this location.

Activating the Power of Heavenly 6 in the Southeast

The number 6, a lucky white star usually associated with the cosmic energies of heaven, flies to the

SE	SOUTH	SW
6 HEAVENLY STAR	2	4
5 (EAST)	7	9 (WEST)
1 NE	3 NORTH	8 NW

Southeast in 2011, directly facing the Northwest, thereby creating a powerful alliance between heaven and earth luck, bringing luck not only to the Southeast but also to the Northwest, directly opposite.

There is great synergy luck between father and eldest daughter in the family. Should either the master bedroom or the daughter's bedroom be located in the Southeast, unexpected developments take place that lift the family fortunes higher than ever. The 6 star brings heaven's celestial blessings and good fortune for those blessed by its cosmic chi. This occurs when your bedroom is located in the Southeast; and if so, do make an effort to fill your room with yang chi energy, a higher noise level and perhaps greater movement in your room. In other words, make it vibrate with energy, as this will energize it, acting as a catalyst for good fortune to occur.

The number 6 signifies authority and power; it is associated with the management of economics and finances. At its peak, 6 stands for authority, influence and control over money, like being the Head of the Central Bank.

Appearing in the Southeast, it suggests financial management does well under a mature woman. Within the family, the year suggests that money should be handled by women and power by men. On balance, however, the male leader has greater strength than the female, but it is the woman who holds the purse strings. This is the way the energies are laid out for the year. Those observing this pattern of energy and flow with it are most likely to benefit from 2011.

It is beneficial to bring this auspicious 6 star to life as it really bring benefits to the entire household, especially in houses where the Southeast is not a tight corner or a small room that locks up its good energy.

To invoke the best kind of results from the 6 star in 2011 display the **Tree of Wealth** in the Southeast. Hang **six large coins** from the tree, and if there are also six birds on the tree, these signify exciting news coming to the household. The best way to create this symbolic effect is to find a healthy growing tree and to place it in the Southeast before hanging all the auspicious symbols that ignite the intrinsic power of 6. Remember, 6 birds and six large coins will attract heaven luck.

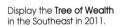

Display the **Tree of Wealth** in the Southeast in 2011.

Enhancing the Tiger's Banner of Victory Luck

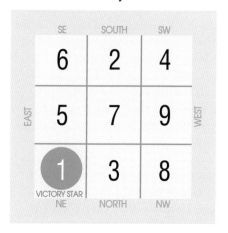

The number 1 star which brings triumph and success flies to the Northeast corner in 2011 and this is also the sector which houses the Tiger. It is thus beneficial for the symbolic banner of victory to be placed here. This also benefits anyone residing in this part of the house for whom this lucky star number brings victory. The number 1 star attracts all kinds of triumphant moments. This kind of luck is especially welcome by those engaged in competitive pursuits, as it helps you win.

In 2011 the Victory Star brings winning luck to young men, especially those who are ambitious and keen to succeed. Those born in the years of the Tiger also benefit from this star number.

What is exciting is that the direction Northeast benefits from three good stars of the 24 mountains, so there is some very exciting potential that can be tapped from this location. It is a good idea to keep the NE energized through the year. Do not let it get too quiet. Yang energy should be created by making sure this part of the house or of your favorite room stays well lit and is occupied. At all costs, prevent *yin spirit formation* by not keeping the sector too silent through the year.

The most auspicious symbols to place here in the Northeast are all the symbols that signify victory such as awards, certificates, trophies and victory banners. You can also fly a flag in the Northeast sector this year. The flag always suggests the announcement of victories.

Benefitting from the Star of Scholarship and Romance in the Southwest

The fourth lucky secondary location of 2011 is the Southwest, which benefits from the romance and scholastic star of 4. This very powerful star will bring beautiful romantic energy to anyone residing in the Southwest.

This is, in any case, the location associated with marriage and domestic happiness. It is also the place of the mother, so the matriarchal force is associated with the Southwest. With the romantic star 4 here, all the stress and strains associated with the *five yellow* of the past year has definitely dissolved.

SE	SOUTH	SW
6	2	4
5	7	9
1	3	8
NE	NORTH	NW

EAST (left side) · WEST (right side)

In 2011, the Southwest brings enhanced love and marriage opportunities. It also brings better harmony and appreciation of the mother figure within families and households.

The number 4 is often associated with romantic peach blossom vibrations, so the luck of this sector directly benefits those still single and unmarried. For those already married, peach blossom brings a happier family life. Domestic energies get enhanced and those who know how to energize the Southwest with bright lights will find the number 4 star jazzing up their love relationships.

Scholastic Luck

Those residing in the Northeast part of the house also benefit from the other influences brought by the number 4 star. These benefits are related to scholastic and literary pursuits, and the star brings good academic luck to those having their bedroom here. Facing Northeast is also beneficial for students and those sitting for examinations. The Northeast stands for wisdom and learning, so this is a very positive star here. The only problem will be that love can also be a distraction, so if you want to enhance the scholastic side of this star, you should place literary symbols here.

Anyone involved in a writing or literary career will also benefit from being located in the Northeast. But do make sure you activate the sector with bright lights. Fire element energy is excellent to add to the strength of the sectors' good luck. Doing so strengthens both the romance as well as the scholastic dimensions of your fortunes in 2011. So light up this corner as best you can!

Magnifying the Earth Element to Enhance Resources

Updating feng shui each year involves more than taking care of lucky and unlucky sectors. It also requires being alert to the balance of elements and their effects on the year's energy flows. This is revealed in the year's four pillars chart which in 2011 indicates an absence of the Earth element in the primary chart of the year. The intrinsic element of the year as indicated by the heavenly stem of the DAY pillar is yang Metal, and altogether there are 3 Metal elements in the chart. There are also three Wood elements, one Water and one Fire, making then a total of the eight elements that make up the primary chart of the year.

Earth element is thus missing in 2011 and the Earth element symbolizes resources. This makes Earth a very important element, because without resources, none of the other indicated attributes such as wealth, success, prosperity, creativity and so forth can manifest.

PAHT CHEE CHART 2011 - GOLDEN RABBIT			
HOUR	DAY	MONTH	YEAR
HEAVENLY STEM	HEAVENLY STEM	HEAVENLY STEM	HEAVENLY STEM
壬	庚	庚	辛
YANG WATER	YANG METAL	YANG METAL	YIN METAL
EARTHLY BRANCH	EARTHLY BRANCH	EARTHLY BRANCH	EARTHLY BRANCH
丙午	甲寅	甲寅	乙卯
FIRE HORSE	WOOD TIGER	WOOD TIGER	WOOD RABBIT
HIDDEN HEAVENLY STEMS OF THE YEAR			
YANG FIRE YANG EARTH	YANG FIRE YANG EARTH YANG WOOD	YANG FIRE YANG EARTH YANG WOOD	YIN WOOD

The year is desperately short of EARTH ie Resource

This is one of the secrets in Paht Chee reading. It is always important that the intrinsic element (in this year, it is Metal) is kept continually replenished by having the element that produces it present. In 2011, this means the Earth element, because Earth produces Metal; hence Earth is the resource element for 2011 - do note that this changes from year to year. As Earth is the missing element this year, it is important that anyone who makes the effort to magnify the presence of Earth element in their living spaces is bound to enjoy excellent feng shui. And Earth element is best symbolized by either a **picture of mountains** or better yet, having the presence of crystals, stones and rocks which come from within the earth.

This is the key that unlocks the manifestation of other kinds of luck for you. It is important to create the presence of Earth element objects in the home and to also strengthen the Earth element corners of the home. These are the Southwest and the Notheast

Keep these corners of the home well lit so that the Fire element is forever present to make these Earth element sectors strong.

The paht chee chart does however show that there is hidden Earth but here the Earth element is not immediately available. Nevertheless, it does indicate the availability of hidden resources. When the Earth element gets magnified the economics of your living situation becomes extremely comfortable.

So do place stones, rocks or crystals - the best are the large circular **crystal globes** - on your coffee table in the living area and then shine a light on it so that the energy of the Earth element gets diffused through the room. Also enhance all compass Earth sectors - Northeast and Southwest as well as the center - in the same way. Creating a "*mountain*" with rocks or pebbles in an artistic way also brings excellent feng shui potential.

Indeed, it is not only the Chinese who have tradition of creating "*miniature mountains*" in and around their gardens and homes. Many other Eastern traditions where feng shui is popularly practiced - such as Japan and Korea - also have their own artistic recreations of mountain scenery. This always signifies the Earth element.

Create a **mountain of pebbles** in your home
to activate the all-important resource element of Earth in 2011.
The NE and SW activated this way brings valuable
hidden resource luck to the home.

Hidden Earth

We need to also look at the entire paht chee chart to
highlight the element that is in most short supply; this
involves looking at all the elements of the year's chart
including the hidden elements. In 2011, there are three
elements of hidden Earth which then brings about a
magnification of the Earth element. But in expanding
the analysis to include the hidden elements, we need to
also take note of the shortage of the Water element. So
as in the previous year, the Water element continues
to be needed. But in this respect, 2011 is better than
2010, because this year there is one Water element
available (last year Water was completely missing). The
Hour pillar has yang Water as its heavenly stem.

> But Water needs to be supplemented to keep the elements in good balance.

Adding to the strength of Water would strengthen to the Wood element for the year and this would be beneficial. This is because Wood symbolizes prosperity and financial success. Hence the placement or addition of the Water element in the Wood sectors East and Southeast would create excellent **wealth feng shui**. Under the Eight Aspirations formula of feng shui, the Southeast is also the sector that stands for prosperity via the accumulation of wealth. To activate this sector, water is required, but water without earth is not as effective as water *with* earth!

So what is required is the placement of a **crystal water feature** in the Southeast corner. This would be an excellent wealth energizer for 2011. Any kind of water presence for this corner in any room that you frequently use (except your bedroom) would be excellent feng shui.

Next place a small image of your own animal sign near the water. This will help you through the year as the presence of water near your sign is symbolically very fruitful. For the Tiger-born, this brings a double benefit because the Tiger's earthly branch is Wood element which gets stronger with water.

Nine Wealth Gods to Materialize Prosperity Luck

The final feng shui tip we would like to share with readers for the year is the placement of a ship bringing nine wealth gods sailing into your home. This has great relevance for the year as it suggests that the winds and waters will bring the divine personifications of wealth luck into the home.

Wealth Gods are a very effective for symbolic placement in feng shui folklore, and it is for this reason that the Chinese always invite Wealth Deities into the home. But there are certain years when the Wealth gods are especially effective and that is when the *Big Auspicious* stars of the 24 mountains fly into two opposite primary directions, which is the case in 2011.

Both the North and the South sectors of every home have, and thus can benefit from these stars; but they work only if they can be energized by the presence of Wealth Deities which are believed to bring good cosmic chi into the homes. This will activate the North-South axis. So do place the ship in a North-South orientation within the home.

Powerful Talismans & Amulets For 2011

Part 7

If you have been following the advice given in these Fortune & Feng Shui books on annual feng shui updates, you are already familiar with the time dimension of feng shui which protects against negative luck each year.

This requires overall cleansing and re-energizing of the energy of the home to prepare for the coming of a new year, while simultaneously making placement changes to accommodate a new pattern of chi distribution. Getting rid of old items and replacing with specially made new remedial cures that are in tune with the year's chi brings pristine and fresh new luck into the home.

The Tiger this year enjoys the Heaven Seal brought by the 24 mountains constellation. This brings you many good opportunities you can seize and turn into something big if you have the luck to do so. You also enjoy Big Auspicious luck, indicating your big break could come this year, as long as the Side Five Yellow hovering nearby does not spoil things for you. In terms of amulets for the year, you thus need to suppress the five yellow, while enhancing your luck from Heaven, to ensure you can fully benefit from whatever big and auspicious is coming your way.

Boost Victory Luck with the Victory Banner Windchime

The Tiger enjoys the number 1 *Victory Star* this year, which occupies your home location of Northeast, making it easy for you to triumph over the competition in any competitive situation you may find yourself in. When you have this kind of luck, it is important to activate with the correct enhancers so this luck does not get wasted. Hang the **Victory Banner Windchime** in the Northeast sector of your home or living room. This will ensure you can overcome any obstacles, enemies, competition, problems and obstructions that come your way, allowing you to focus your energies on tapping the luck of *Big Auspicious*.

Attract Mentor Support & Heaven Luck with the Heaven Seal Activator

The Heaven Seal star sits directly in your Tiger direction this year, bringing you precious luck from above. Activate this auspicious luck with a Heaven Seal Activator, which has been specially designed with the image of the Jade Emperor of Heaven, while on the reverse side engraved with the Chien Trigram, bringing you wealth, success and prosperity luck "as *vast as the skies*". Carry this seal with you through the year will bring you the support of powerful people, boost mentor luck for you, as well as attract opportunities, recognition and wealth.

Suppress the Jealousy of Others with the Anti-Evil-Eye Hanging

When you enjoy a lot of success, you could attract the jealousy of others, especially your peers and those in direct competition with you. This could well be the case for the Tiger in 2011 and thus it is important for you to stay well protected by carrying the **Anti-Evil-Eye Hanging**. Even when one enjoys superlative wealth luck and career success, it is stressful and no fun at all when others harbor negative thoughts about you, hope for your downfall, or covet what you have at your expense. When your luck is too good, it becomes even more important to stay protected. The anti-evil-eye hanging prevents others from turning against you when they start to envy what you have, transforming any negative thoughts into well wishes. This will make your life a lot more peaceful and pleasant this year, allowing you to enjoy your triumphant moments to the fullest.

Actualize Big Success with the Crystal Water Talisman

Water is the element that is terribly lacking in the 2011 Paht Chee chart, and carrying a symbol of Water with you attracts big luck to you. This is especially the case for the Tiger person, who can tap the luck of *Big Auspicious* this year. Having this element with you at all times is sure to add potency to your success luck, allowing good opportunities to translate into results for you. This talisman will also fuel your self element of Wood, strengthening you personally.

Subdue the Side Five Yellow with the Five Element Pagoda

The Tiger is indirectly afflicted by the Side Five Yellow affliction this year, which although not as dangerous as when it sits directly in your location, can nevertheless be a source of unneccesary stress, headaches and heartaches. It is thus a good idea to suppress this with a Five Element Pagoda, the best cure against this troublesome star. You can wear one around your neck as a pendant to be personally protected wherever you go. You should also display one with the Tree of Life in the East sector of your home and office. The Five Element Pagoda decorated with the Tree of Life growing from its base turns this feng shui cure into a powerful wealth enhancing tool, allowing you to transform any negative energies into positive ones.

Make Best Use of Positive Affirmations to Unleash the Power of your Subconscious

Positive words, sayings and affirmations when viewed over and over are like mantras that enter your subconscious. We have incorporated these affirmative and positive sayings into several of our new items this year as powerful activators of good luck. The Tiger person should give strength to their Big Luck this year by carrying the "*Lucky*" keychain. Using, handling and exposing yourself to this word over and over can have a tremendous effect on how your luck pans out this year.

The glass pebbles and mandala stones with positive words and auspicious symbols have the same effect, and can be displayed in your animal sign location of Northeast for best effect. Choose stones with words or pictures that hold special meaning for you. Put them ina pot or bowl in the Northeast, or even better, load them onto a miniature sailing ship, letting the ship sail in from one of your good directions. You can also add these stones into your mandala offering set, if you have one.

Sacred Moving Mantra Watches

Moving mantra watches are suitable for any animal sign; anyone can wear them. These watches have been specially designed to bring you the trinity of luck - heaven, earth and mankind luck. There are 3 clocks in this watch, so it can support 3 time zones, but even better, around each dial is a mantra which moves, so every second that passes is like chanting an auspicious mantra. The mantras featured on this watch are the Amitabha Buddha mantra, Manjushri mantra and the Kuan Yin mantra. Wearing this watch will bring you preotection and attract you plenty of good fortune and prosperity continuously through the day and night.

Also available this year are the Medicine Buddha **watch** and the Green Tara watch. The **Medicine**

Buddha watch has been specially designed to bring you good health and it comes with the Medicine Buddha mantra and image. The band is embossed with the Medicine Buddha mantra. The mantra is repeated on the face in a moving dial, so the mantra is constantly moving. Wearing this watch will bring you good health and protection from sickness. Suitable for those of you who may be prone to falling sick, or the more elderly Tiger to maintain good health and a long, happy and comfortable life.

The **Green Tara watch** features the beautiful Green Tara in the face. The band of the watch is stamped with the Green Tara mantra - Om Tare Tuttare Ture Soha - and this mantra is repeated in a dial on the face which is constantly moving, creating blessings for you all hours of the night and day. Green Tara brings success luck and helps you to overcome blocks and obstacles to success. She is also known as the Swift Liberator, known to bring results quickly to those who call on her help.

Table Top Treasures to Enhance Desks and Workspaces

Many of us spend a great deal of our time at our desks and in front of our computers whether during work, play or our spare time. It is always good to energize the immediate space around us with good fortune symbols and items that hold positive meaning for us. We have designed two such items that make simply the most delightful table top treasures, a **miniature photo frame** enameled with peonies, the flower of love, and a **matching clock**. Place photos of your loved ones in such photo frames near you while you work. This will bring you positive and happy energy, and when you're happy, you become more productive, more peaceful and yes, also more lucky.

Powerful Gemstones to Connect Your Lucky Day with the Seven Most Powerful Planets

The seven planets signify seven days of the week, and connection with each planet is achieved by wearing its correct gemstone. Using your lucky day of the week, you can determine which planet has the luckiest influence on you and which gemstone you should wear or carry close to your body to attract the good luck of that planet. Start wearing the gem on your lucky day and empower with incense and mantras before wearing.

The SUN is the planet of Sunday

This is the principal planet which gives light and warmth, brings fame and recognition and enhances one's personal aura. It is an empowering planet that brings nobility, dignity and power. This gemstone enhances your leadership qualities and increases your levels of confidence so your mind is untroubled and clear. The color that activates the SUN is RED, so all red-colored gemstones are excellent for those of you having SUNDAY as your lucky day based on your Lunar Mansion.

Rubies, red garnets, rubellites or even **red glass** or **crystal** would be extremely powerful. You can also wear red clothes, carry red handbags to enhance the energy of the Sun, but a red gemstone is the most powerful... Start wearing on a Sunday at sunrise after reciting the mantra here 7 times.

Mantra: *Om Grini Suraya Namah Hum Phat*

The MOON is the planet of Monday

The moon has a powerful influence on your mind, your thoughts and attitudes. Lunar energy is associated with the tides and with water, bringing enormous good fortune to those who successfully activate its positive influences; and is especially suitable for those whose lucky day is Monday.

For energizing lunar energy, the best is to wear the pearl, those created in the deep seas or from the freshwater of rivers. Wearing pearls (any color) bring good habits to the wearer and creates good thoughts. It brings calm, peace of mind, mental stability and good health. It also brings wealth and enhances all positive thoughts. Over time, it engenders the respect of others. Start wearing on a Monday in the evening before sunset and recite the mantra here 11 times.

Mantra: *Om Som Somaya Namah Hum Phat*

The Planet MARS rules Tuesday

This is a masculine planet associated with fiery energy and the power of oratory. Activating Mars brings an authoritative air of leadership and confidence like a general leading troops to war. It brings success and victory in any competitive situation. Worn on a Tuesday, a gemstone that resonates with Mars unleashes all its fiery strength in competitive situations. The most powerful gemstone to activate Mars is **natural red coral**, the deeper the red, the better it will be. Start wearing on a Tuesday one hour after sunrise and after reciting the mantra here 19 times.

Mantra: *Om Ang Anghara Kaya Namah Hum Phat*

The Planet MERCURY rules Wednesdays

To anyone who can successfully activate Mercury, this planet brings great intelligence and amazing analytical capabilities that become vastly enhanced. Mercury increases your ability to learn and your powers of absorption are magnified. The ability to memorize also improves. Mercury facilitates powers of expression and communication. You will work fast and become effective in getting things done. The cosmic color of Mercury is green; **emeralds, green** tourmalines, green quartz are all suitable. **Green jade** is the most powerful energizer of Mercury. Anyone wearing jade will always be smarter than others and can always outwit anyone. It is a very powerful gemstone. Start wearing on a Wednesday two hours after sunrise and recite the mantra here 9 times.

Mantra: *Om Bhrum Buddhaya Namah Hum Phat*

The Planet Jupiter rules Thursdays

The most auspicious of the seven planets, this planet attracts wealth and brings great influence to those who can successfully activate its powerful energies. To do so requires you to perform many charitable works and then you will need to wear the gemstone of Jupiter that will make you rise to spectacular heights of success. You will become a highly respected leader wielding power and great influence.

Jupiter's energies are transmitted through yellow gemstones the most powerful of which are **yellow sapphires, citrines, topaz** or **flawless yellow-coloured glass** or **crystal**. Wear a yellow sapphire that is flawless and is at least 7 carats big. This brings enormous wealth luck. **Yellow Citrines** or **Imperial Topaz** are also effective. But they must be flawless or you will be quick-tempered and hard to please. Start wearing on a Thursday an hour before sunset after reciting the mantra here 19 times.

Mantra: *Om Bhrim Bhrihas Pataye Namah Hum Phat*

The Planet Venus rules Fridays

This is the planet of love, romance, sexuality, marriage, material comforts, domestic bliss and luxury. Venus brings all kinds of artistic skills to those whose lucky day is Friday and also to those who empower Venus by connecting to it via the wearing of its gemstones. Venus transmits its cosmic energy through **flawless diamonds, quartz crystals, zircons, white sapphires,** and other **colorless gemstones** with **clear transparency.**

Various subtle hues such as pink, yellow and blue tints are suitable for different types of professions and social positions, as long as the gem does not have any solid color. So it is crystalline stones that resonate best with Venus. Start wearing on a Friday at sunrise after you recite the mantra here 16 times.

Mantra: *Om Shum Shukraya Namah Hum Phat*

The Planet Saturn rules Saturdays

This planet governs careers and an empowered or energized Saturn is excellent for overcoming obstacles at the work place. When projects or bosses cause you to stumble or when hindrances stand in the way, it is because Saturn has to be appeased. Those whose lucky day is Friday possess the ability to rise above hardships and obstacles, but enhancing Saturn by wearing its gemstone will empower you even more. Anyone wearing **Blue Sapphires** can connect directly with Saturn.

Start wearing on a Saturday 2 and a half hours before sunset and recite the mantra here 23 times.

Mantra: *Om Sham Shanay Scaraya Namah Hum Phat*

So, What Do You Think?

We hope you enjoyed this book and gained some
meaningful insights about your own personal
horoscope and animal sign... and you've put some
of our feng shui recommendations into practice!
Hopefully you are already feeling a difference
and enjoying the results of the positive actions
you have taken.

But Don't Stop Now!

You can receive the latest weekly news and
feng shui updates from Lillian herself absolutely
FREE! Learn even more of her secrets and
open your mind to the deeper possibilities of
feng shui today.

Lillian too's free online weekly ezine is
now AVAILABLE

Here's how easy it is to subscribe:
Just go online to www.lilliantoomandalaezine.com
and sign up today!

Your newsletter will be delivered automatically to your website.

And there's more!

When you subscribe to my FREE Mandala Weekly Ezine you will receive a special personalized BONUS report from me... but it's only available for those who register online at www.lilliantoomandalaezine.com!

DON'T BE LEFT OUT! Join Today!

Thank you for investing in yourself and in this book. Join me online every week and learn how easy it is to make good feng shui a way of life!